Marketing Women's Health Care

Ruthie H. Dearing, MHSA, JD
President and Hospital Consultant
Dearing & Associates, Incorporated
Spokane, Washington

Helen A. Gordon, RN, MS
Director of Women-Infant Services
Wake Medical Center
Raleigh, North Carolina

Dorolyn M. Sohner, RN, BSN
Senior Consultant
Dearing & Associates, Incorporated
Spokane, Washington

Lynne C. Weidel, MHA
Senior Consultant
Dearing & Associates, Incorporated
Spokane, Washington

AN ASPEN PUBLICATION®
Aspen Publishers, Inc.
Rockville, Maryland
Royal Tunbridge Wells
1987

Library of Congress Cataloging-in-Publication Data

Marketing women's health care.

"An Aspen publication."
Includes bibliographies and index.
1. Women's health services—United States—Marketing.
2. Maternal health services—United States—Marketing.
I. Dearing, Ruthie H. [DNLM: 1. Marketing of Health
Services. 2. Maternal Health Services. WA 310 M345]
RA564.85.M39   1987   362.1'98'0688   86-30223
ISBN: 0-87189-633-8

Editorial Services: Ruth Bloom

Library of Congress Catalog Card Number: 86-30223
ISBN: 0-87189-633-8

Printed in the United States of America

1 2 3 4 5

Table of Contents

Preface

Marketing Women's Health Care is the culmination of numerous experiences with health care providers working to distinguish their organization in today's competitive marketplace. Because women are the primary users of health care and the major decision makers regarding health care choices for the entire family, almost all administrators recognize that appealing to this market is one strategy to distinguish their hospital. Our consulting efforts have primarily focused on assisting health care providers to successfully attract and hold this market.

Much has been written about applying business marketing techniques and strategies to the health care field. We have attempted to bring a fresh perspective by taking established theories and reforming them to more effectively match the demands faced by health care providers today. The material is structured to provide guidelines from development to operational reality of new and updated programs in women's health care.

The authors wish to acknowledge, with much gratitude, the untiring and splendid assistance provided by Judith Puckett, our Administrative Assistant. We also wish to thank the skunk, who appeared during the final day of frantic manuscript editing, for adding a special essence and excitement to the overall project.

Part I

Marketing Redefined

Chapter 1

What Is Marketing?

1

In today's client-driven health care market, the development of a marketing plan and marketing strategies is essential. An important market segment, one long overlooked, is now gaining the attention of health care providers throughout the country. Women, who make up the majority of the population, have become the focus of all health care marketers, providers, and product developers.

Marketing oriented to women appears to many hospitals as a panacea for resolving declining census and patient acquisition problems. We do not believe marketing to women can solve all problems, but it can make a significant difference in a hospital's ability to attract patients and maintain patient relationships. However, like other marketing, it must be planned and executed thoughtfully, with sensitivity to individual provider environments. In order to accomplish this successfully, an understanding of marketing concepts and fundamentals is necessary.

MARKETING DEFINED

Marketing is probably one of the most misunderstood and misused concepts in the health care industry today. It is often confused with public relations or sales. Yet there are distinct differences between public relations, sales, and marketing.

Public relations concentrates on publications and news, while marketing includes tools of promotion and generally involves many different activities. Marketing brings in planning, testing, research and analysis, targeting, and strategy development, all of which depend on the interaction between an organization and its communities.

Philip Kotler, one of the first to apply marketing principles to health care, defines marketing as "the analysis, planning, implementation and control of carefully formulated programs designed to bring about voluntary exchanges of value with target markets for the purpose of achieving organizational objectives."[1]

Because this definition is long and complex, it must be examined closely in order to understand its meaning and application. Marketing, Kotler says, is "for the purpose of achieving organizational objectives." It is the implementation of objectives, i.e., doing what the hospital sets out to do. Marketing is not a goal in and of itself. It is part of a total effort to accomplish the goals and objectives selected by an organization, goals that define its business and direct its course of action. However, because marketing is new to health care providers, it appears at times to become the goal, rather than merely being a part of the overall effort to accomplish organizational goals. Successful marketing can never be achieved if the proper perspective about its purpose is not maintained.

Marketing can be used to bring services, products, and organizations to the attention of a specific public. This is one of the goals the health care provider is seeking to achieve when marketing individual services. When the Kotler definition is applied to a specific service like maternity care, the objective becomes to plan for and provide certain benefits (family-centered maternity care, mother-baby nursing, and sibling visits) for a specific public (expectant patients), with the additional purpose of supporting (by increased volume) the organization (hospital).

In the mind of many health care managers, marketing and sales are identical. However, selling is actually only one component of the overall marketing process. A good definition that clearly explains the difference between marketing and selling has been provided by Theodore Levitt. He says that selling tries to get the customer to want what the company has, while marketing tries to get the company to have what the customer wants.[2] The latter is what has been done in hospitals that have changed traditional obstetric departments into innovative family-centered maternity care programs.

Another example of this is the hospital that creates an attractive, supportive women's inpatient unit, after learning from its community that traditional inpatient care is not what today's women want. A hospital making such changes is clearly doing what Levitt describes: getting the hospital (company) to have what the patient (customer) wants, as opposed to getting the patient to want what the hospital has. This is more than selling; this is marketing.

The foundation of all marketing is exchange. Simply put, this means when a hospital and a patient come together in the marketplace, each has something to offer that the other wants. If a transaction is completed, it is implied that there is a sufficient degree of satisfaction for both parties. Hopefully the transaction results in equal benefits to both parties. Equality of benefit should be a primary goal of a hospital's marketing effort.

Applying this to the maternity care example, expectant parents receive care according to their needs and desires: a family-oriented birth, with personalized mother-baby nursing and sibling involvement. In exchange, the parents give what the hospital wants: word-of-mouth praise for this special care, a relationship tying the family to the hospital, and payment for services. The precise method of exchange, matched appropriately with a target market or distinct public, distinguishes the marketing process from the particular functions of public relations, advertising, and sales.

MARKETING COMPONENTS

The marketing process is divided into several components:

- research
- analysis
- strategy development
- product line development
- promotion and advertising
- evaluation

Each component contributes distinctly to the total marketing process. Side-stepping or short-changing any one component may endanger the successful outcome. Because of the many components, a wide variety of people at many different levels, both inside and outside the organization, may need to participate in the process in order to achieve the marketing goals.

The components of marketing are defined below.

Research

This component of the marketing process is essential as a first step. Research includes reviewing demographic data; gathering opinion data through questionnaires, surveys, and interviews; concept testing; competitive analysis; and assessing regulatory issues. The purpose of research is to provide quantifiable and measurable data.

Analysis

Analysis involves a thorough review of all data gathered and the formation of conclusions. The purpose is to interpret the findings, enabling management to make objective, thoughtful decisions about the needs and desires of the hospital's consumers.

Strategy Development

This component primarily involves management decision making. During this phase, management translates the results of the market research and analysis into a plan of action for the entire organization, as well as for individual programs and services. Translation must reflect a big picture approach and adapt national trends, both on an institutional and a local level. The purpose of strategy development is to create a vehicle which promotes the accomplishment of the organization's overall goals. This phase of the total marketing process is structured to produce a written marketing plan and budget.

Product Line Development

Product line development includes the creation of new services and the refinement of existing ones. This is done by utilizing the information obtained from the research, analysis, and strategy development phases of the marketing process. The purpose of product line development is to design the services and programs offered by the organization so that they are responsive to consumers and well received by hospital staff. Many professionals within the organization contribute to this activity. Responsibility for program design rests with those who will deliver the service or program. Marketing staff contribute by providing marketing research data that affect program design. Marketing staff also assist with the packaging, promotion, and sales activities needed to sell the product.

Promotion and Advertising

These closely related functions, both part of the total marketing process, are often thought to be all there is to marketing. Actually, the promotion and advertising functions are merely the most visible of the many components of the marketing process. The purpose of these two functions is to further the acceptance and sale of services offered by the hospital or other health care provider. Advertising brings a particular service to the attention of the public primarily through paid announcements. Promotions focus on special events or activities designed to attract public interest.

Evaluation

The final component in the marketing process is one with a dual focus. Evaluation of individual programs and services implemented through the product line development phase must occur regularly. At the same time, the results of all marketing efforts must be continually measured against the targets estimated for the overall organization during the strategy development phase.

The major purpose of evaluation is to determine if marketing outcomes match marketing expectations. A secondary purpose of evaluation and program review is to verify results, thereby justifying continued or additional funding.

PURPOSE AND VALUE OF MARKETING

As evident to all health care providers, the delivery of health care services has changed markedly over the past decade. No longer can a hospital rest on its reputation and past accomplishments, taking for granted that consumers, both patients and physicians, will choose it simply because they did so in the past.

From the patient's perspective, one hospital appears no different from another. Because patients are unable to adequately assess the quality of clinical care, they usually assume all hospitals provide comparable care. Yet, coupled with the patient's perception that all hospitals provide good care is a desire and demand for more than that.

Today's patients evaluate clinical care using a number of non-technical criteria that are often completely foreign to the providers. For example, many patients equate good care with cleanliness, friendliness of the staff, and individualized patient care, without considering the technical or clinical skills of the caregivers. This creates a need among hospitals to portray an image consistent with these desired characteristics in order to attract patients. Also, the growing number of alternative providers has further intensified competition for patients. In response to these pressures, marketing has become an essential tool in the institution's overall strategy for survival.

An effective marketing program can accomplish a number of goals. These goals include:

- providing valuable information about consumer need and demand to aid in the refinement of existing services and development of new ones
- creating a focus for hospital resources
- facilitating thoughtful, educated decision making
- providing the public with a means to distinguish one facility from another

- learning of gaps in service, both internal and external
- increasing visibility and awareness among consumers, especially for a particular program or service

Why Market to Women?

For the past several decades, other consumer product industries have recognized the impact and influence women have on purchasing decisions. From extensive marketing research, the clothing, food, and household goods industries learned long ago that women were responsible for a substantial majority of the decisions effecting purchases. As a result, each of these industries has spent millions of dollars developing sophisticated marketing campaigns directed at women. Until recently, the health care industry had little need or desire to conduct marketing research or marketing campaigns.

Today, however, the health care industry also has become aware of the impact of the sheer number of women in this country on the marketplace and recognized the need to take their impact into account. Indeed, statistics indicate that women are the major users of health care services:

- Women are admitted to hospitals more frequently than men. Even factoring out childbirth, the number of female admissions is fifteen percent higher than those for males.[3]
- Women account for sixty-three percent of all adult surgeries performed in hospitals. Of the twenty most frequently performed surgical procedures for those under sixty-five years of age, eleven are performed exclusively on women.[4]
- Almost forty percent of ambulatory surgeries are GYN procedures. When added to other outpatient surgeries performed on women, women account for the majority of ambulatory surgical procedures.[5]
- Women are more likely to have a chronic illness needing regular care. Eighty-three percent of women (compared to seventy-three percent of men) regularly go to the same physician.

Perhaps even more important, recent consumer surveys conducted by both the National Research Corporation (NRC), Lincoln,

Nebraska, and Dearing & Associates, Spokane, Washington, indicate that women are responsible for the majority of health care purchasing decisions, not just for themselves, but for their families. Also:

- Women make the selection of hospital six out of ten times for the treatment of illness or injuries.
- Women are four times more likely than men to select a health care provider for treatment of a child.
- Women select physicians almost twice as often as do men. Surveys indicate that women choose fifty-three percent of regular physicians, while men choose only twenty-eight percent.
- Women select physicians for their own care eighty percent of the time while men select physicians for themselves fifty-six percent of the time. Husbands are more likely to consult their wives on the choice of physician than wives are likely to consult their husbands.
- Women most frequently rely upon the advice of friends when selecting a new physician. The recommendation of her current physician is a close second.
- Fifty-eight percent of pregnant women choose a hospital first, and a physician second, for maternity care.
- The average pregnant woman calls or visits three hospitals before selecting where she will deliver.
- Women do travel outside their community for health care. NRC research shows that eighty-eight percent of women are willing to drive thirty minutes for women's programs or services. Market research conducted by Dearing & Associates across the country indicates that women travel (sometimes for as long as one hour) for services they perceive to be better or unavailable than those closer to home.

Women are also more likely than men to be informed about and actively participate in health care services. According to the NRC survey results:

- Forty percent of female consumers recall health care advertising.

- Newspaper advertising is most frequently remembered by female consumers. Television advertising is second, followed by direct mail. Radio ads are least frequently remembered.

- More women (twenty-five percent) regularly read articles about health care than do men (eleven percent).

- Women are interested in learning about health care options. Twenty-six percent of women are very interested in receiving material regularly from hospitals on programs and services. Only sixteen percent of men show this same degree of interest.

- Women (twenty-four percent) are more likely than men (sixteen percent) to take part in health education and wellness programs.

These statistics demonstrate the magnitude of health care dollars generated from the treatment of women. Hospitals are actively involved in attempts to retain former patients and attract new ones. Because women are greater users of health care, it is obvious that hospitals can benefit by directing marketing efforts at women.

Further evidence of the sway women have over health care purchasing decisions is found in recent studies showing that sixty-seven percent of all health care decisions are made or influenced by women.[6] The opinion of family or friends has long been recognized as a strong influence on the choice of a hospital or a physician. Women often function as a triage officer would, providing information and directing family members to particular hospitals or health care providers.

Obviously, long-term relationships with families are the ultimate goal of any health care provider. Because of women's heavy use of health care services and their influence over choices of providers for family members, women are the key persons at whom marketing should be directed. For example, market research shows that thirty-eight percent of all families have their first experience with a hospital through the maternity care service.[7] This experience, if positive, creates a powerful first impression which can be the beginning of a long-term relationship with a family.

The authors' experience working with hospitals of all sizes has demonstrated the benefit of marketing research in refining existing programs and developing new product lines designed to appeal to women. These experiences have shown how effective, well-executed marketing campaigns directed specifically at women can increase volume and assist with patient acquisition.

Hospitals and other health care providers have begun to realize the importance of marketing and the potential of the women's market. However, because of the complexity of the marketing function and the often fragmented approach in using it, few hospitals have fully mastered the art of marketing. Research findings from NRC confirm this conclusion. Only one in four women is aware of specialized women's services. Further, one-third of women do not know what services are offered in a specialized women's program. Clearly, health care providers must attain greater marketing skills if they are to realize the full potential of the women's health care market.

NOTES

1. Philip Kotler, *Marketing for Non-Profit Organizations* (Englewood Cliffs, N.J.: Prentice-Hall, 1975).

2. Theodore Levitt, *The Marketing Imagination* (New York, N.Y.: The Free Press, 1983).

3. Cynthia Wallace, "Women's Healthcare Spending, New Target of Hospital Ads," *Modern Healthcare,* March 15, 1985, p. 52.

4. *Ibid.*

5. "Maternity Services Shift in Response to Consumer Demand," *Hospitals,* April 16, 1985, p. 88.

6. Joe Inquanzo and Mark Harju, "Creating a Market Niche," *Hospitals,* January 1, 1985.

7. National Research Corporation, Lincoln, Neb., 1986.

Chapter 2

Components of a Marketing Plan

2

The marketing plan is a written guideline based upon decisions made during the strategy development phase. It includes some of the components of the marketing process as well as other components specific to the plan. This document serves as a blueprint for the hospital staff as they implement their ideas and create an operating program.

The components of a marketing plan are:

1. background data

   - market research and analysis
   - review of regulatory issues
   - competitive analysis
   - demographic data
   - financial review
   - national trends applied to the local situation

2. identification of target markets
3. segmentation of target markets
4. establishment of goals and objectives
5. identification of provider resources that support the goals and objectives
6. development of the promotion and advertising approach

7. evaluation and measurement of outcomes against targets estimated in the goals.

The authors have found that a one year time frame for the marketing plan provides an effective period for accomplishing goals. One
year is adequate to obtain results, yet does not cause the plan to be
outdated due to environmental changes. As with the marketing
process, many staff members participate in program and action
plan development. A member of the management team should be
given responsibility for organizing and directing the marketing plan
development activities. This individual can form a marketing plan
team or committee from internal hospital staff in the following
departments:

• marketing
• public relations
• planning
• development
• administration

In addition to these staff members, we recommend involving
members of the caregivers management team from the particular
service being marketed. Also, board of trustee members, consultants, representatives from public relations or advertising agencies,
and opinion leaders in the women's community are good additions
to the team or committee. Generally a separate marketing program
and action plan are prepared for each service or group of services.
Marketing programs and action plans should be constantly
reviewed and revised to accommodate changes.

MARKET AREA ANALYSIS

Market area analysis is the term frequently given to a market
research and analysis project. As mentioned in Chapter 1, a market
area analysis is a necessary first step in the marketing process.

In the past, program decisions involving new development or program refinement were made in part for the following reasons:

- Key physician admitter wanted a new service to be offered.
- Administrators, relying on their perceptions of the market, believed they knew the services patients wanted and would use.
- The hospital played catch up with the competition by duplicating existing or newly developed services.
- An employee or member of the medical staff had some special expertise.
- The administrator's ego needed to be bolstered.

Market area analysis changes all of this. It provides an objective overview of the hospital's environment, which can then be combined with management's subjective perspectives to respond to the market more effectively. As the health care field continues to change, with roller coaster effects on both the national and local level, market research provides a means of monitoring changes and their occurrence in a particular hospital's service area.

For example, if a competitor opens an innovative maternity care unit, invests $100,000 on marketing and promotional activity, and conducts an open house with 2500 community residents in attendance, the awareness and knowledge level of all consumers in the surrounding communities will be changed. Maternity care patients, in particular, will view the hospital making the changes—and all other hospitals—from an entirely new perspective. And even though another hospital may have previously been the leader in obstetrics volume and had the best reputation, when a competitor begins marketing an innovative, patient-oriented program, past beliefs and use patterns can diminish or change quickly.

Other patients with no interest in maternity care will also be influenced by the marketing/promotional campaign of the competitor. Usually the reputation of an entire hospital is enhanced by innovative programming in one area, which causes a shift in public perception about the facility's overall capability and status in the community. This shift in perceptions can occur in an incredibly short time.

For example, a small community hospital, with an obstetrics volume between one thousand and twelve hundred deliveries per year, renovated its service and began an advertising and marketing campaign in the surrounding communities. The small hospital's main competitor was a large community teaching hospital with an annual obstetrical volume of approximately five thousand deliveries. Initially, only a handful of the large hospital's obstetrical staff of over forty members had privileges at the small hospital or even considered using the facility. Within two months of opening, the small hospital's newly renovated maternity care unit was drawing forty to fifty patients a month from the large hospital's low-risk, private-paying patient population. In addition, every member of the obstetrical attending staff at the large hospital had requested privileges and followed his or her patients to the smaller facility.

This is not an uncommon situation today. Many hospitals, both large and small, face the challenges described above, either attempting to attract patients or working frantically to keep them. Often the administration or medical staff of a large hospital may be reluctant to change or, if they do decide to change, organizational structure and size require a long time for implementation of the changes. Not infrequently, a large hospital will have been lulled into complacency by volume, high-tech capabilities, or past patient and physician use patterns.

One of the first rules of business and marketing applies here: Never overlook or underestimate any competitor! Strengths that a hospital previously relied on to attract patients or physicians may no longer be what either consumer is now seeking. Market area analysis provides the mechanism for the hospital to stay in touch with the needs and likes of consumers—both patients and physicians. This allows the hospital to operate from a proactive position, rather than a reactive one.

Another reason to invest in market research and analysis involves the medical staff and board. For years, the obstetric service has been overlooked or thought to be a financial drain on the hospital. Often, little if any resources have been expended on program or physical plant changes. This has recently become extremely frustrating to many obstetricians, who are aware of the correlation between maternity care and the development of long-term relationships with families.

Many publications and newspapers read by physicians speak of the importance of market research and analysis as the basis for new program development. As the women's health care movement grows, physicians become concerned if their primary hospital is not using these tools to study its market and react to changes in consumer demand. Well-informed physicians are aware of patients choosing one hospital over another for maternity care and other specially designed women's programs. If the hospital chosen is not one where a given physician practices, he or she will be angry at the loss of patients to competing physicians.

Conversely, if the medical staff is reluctant to change, market area analysis data can be an effective means of convincing both medical staff and board members of the need for new services. Not only are objective, quantifiable data available to substantiate need and demand, but management's credibility is enhanced by demonstrating thoughtful, well-researched decision making.

Outcomes Common to All Hospitals

Expected outcomes of market area analysis clearly demonstrate how deficiencies in previous decision making are overcome. Obviously, some of the expected outcomes in market research and analysis are highly individualized and occur only for particular facilities. However, there are several outcomes resulting from market area analysis that are common to all hospitals. These common outcomes are:

1. provision of an objective basis for decision making among competing product lines
2. provision of a comprehensive and common understanding of the marketplace among all involved in or concerned with the project, including the market plan development team or committee, top administration, and the medical staff
3. identification of potential roadblocks to new program development

4. provision of specific information describing the prospective patient population:

- number and distribution of women in various age cohorts (information based on hard data rather than assumptions formed from historical use patterns)
- patient opinions and attitudes (information based on what patients say and think, rather than on what hospital staff think they think)

5. knowledge of an individual facility's position in relation to other hospitals and health care facilities providing a particular service

Health care providers have a tendency to interpret health care data in a traditional manner, assuming that past utilization patterns and historical behavior will continue unchanged into the future. Even when change is acknowledged, it is viewed with a myopic perspective, coupled with a tendency to discount the effects change can have on a particular institution.

An unexpected, but observable, outcome of market area analysis is the benefit a hospital derives from making the effort to gather data and consumer opinions about providers and services. Frequently, women participating in a survey will comment about how pleased they are to have the opportunity to give information for consideration by a hospital. Many women mention that a market assessment in itself enhances their opinion of the hospital responsible for it.

Who Should Do the Market Research?

More and more health care facilities are turning to outside organizations specializing in marketing research and analysis to assist with the marketing process. This raises the dilemma about what portion of the market area analysis can be done by in-house staff and what portion should be done by an outside firm. Two factors usually surface: the bias of in-house staff versus the outside consultant's unfamiliarity with the hospital's environment. The bias of in-house staff seems to be the more difficult factor to overcome. Generally, in-house staff function most effectively with those portions of the market area analysis that are technical in nature. Because in-house staff want to, and often do, believe their institution is the "best," it is difficult for them to "hear" objectively the information consumers provide. In-house staff can beneficially conduct the review of patient origin data, population trends, and regulatory issues, but an outside firm is better positioned to handle the data involving more complex interpretation, such as public opinion surveys, physician and board interviews, concept testing, competitor assessment, and image assessment. However, all portions of a market area analysis can be done by an outside consulting firm or organization if desired.

One of the most important factors to consider in the selection of an outside firm is whether a given firm has special expertise and knowledge of a particular service or program. Such expertise gives a consultant an understanding and sensitivity to the broader market issues that must be addressed in order for a program to be successful. General marketing consultants without special knowledge may have good analytical skills, but can overlook subtleties or nuances in data that affect the interpretation of and conclusions drawn from the data. Because women's health care is so new, it is also unlikely that in-house staff will have the special expertise an outside firm can bring to a particular project. The in-house staff may well have the technical skills to gather and organize data, but it is useful to have outside consultants assist with interpretation.

Another factor to consider when choosing an outside firm is whether a potential consultant is able to understand the interplay between the program with which they are involved and the other programs and services that are a priority for the hospital. Consultants have a tendency to forget the hospital is involved with programs and projects other than the one with which they are working. Program plans or recommendations that do not take into account relevant related issues will not benefit any facility.

Often what seems to be the "best" plan is too idealistic or unrealistic to allow implementation. Best has a very broad definition and requires consideration of multiple factors and issues. Finally, a related attribute focuses on the ability to bring one program smoothly into an overall marketing plan and budget. Because of the limited resources with which all hospitals are operating, priorities for marketing resources (both people and dollars) must be carefully evaluated. It is sometimes difficult for consultants working on only one program to recognize the limitations under which the entire marketing plan and budget must operate. However, if they do recognize this, their expertise in evaluating where to expand marketing efforts, in light of limited resources, often is very helpful. The key is to make certain the consultants clearly understand the priorities and work within the hospital's budget and overall plan.

The consultant's ability to set the stage for change by building enthusiasm and support among hospital staff for new program development is essential and desirable. This is a most beneficial skill, which if used properly can create positive motivation for program implementation. If misused, program development and implementation can be sidetracked.

Finally, in order to become familiar with the style and effectiveness of a consulting firm, it is essential to verify its past performance by contacting previous clients. Inquiries to previous clients should focus not only on the process used by the firm, but also on the outcome and results of the work performed.

How To Use the Information

The primary use for the information generated from a market area analysis is to determine program feasibility. If the program is feasible, the information serves as a guide for program design. It can help answer questions as to what services should be offered and how, when, and where services should be delivered.

In gathering, reviewing, and analyzing the data, it is essential to clearly distinguish between consumer interest and desire for a program to be developed and consumer willingness to use the program or service once developed. Research has repeatedly shown that a smaller number of women indicate a willingness to use a service than the number who think the same service should be provided. When women are questioned about this noticeable difference in response, the most common answer is that it is desirable to have the service available in case it is needed.

Market area analysis information is also valuable in identifying target markets for the new service. The information is helpful in determining major barriers to program implementation, allowing strategies for overcoming them to be developed early in the planning process. Market analysis often will uncover unknown supporters or opponents, assisting administration to prevent a ninth-hour crisis. And as mentioned earlier, the information can be an invaluable tool useful in convincing board members, medical staff, and regulatory agencies of the appropriateness or inappropriateness of the project.

Identifying Your Public

In the past, when health care providers planned health care services for women patients, the services developed were primarily either maternity care or traditional gynecological surgery services. However with our aging population and the diminishing number of births, hospitals that focus attention only on services relating to reproduction are missing a major patient acquisition opportunity.

Today, all women are potential patients. Hospitals and other health care providers must work to capture this market with a broader range of programs and more specialized services that women of all ages and backgrounds are seeking. Opportunities clearly exist for the provider in tune with the health care needs and desires of women in the 1980s.

In order to increase market share, it is important to design programs that are highly responsive to the needs and expectations of consumers. Although all women are potential users of a program or service, individual needs and desires vary significantly. Differences among women are based on the following:

- age
- health status
- socioeconomic status
- employment or occupation
- motherhood
- marital status
- ethnic and cultural background

- education
- religion
- geography

Market segmentation is a method of dividing a large target population into homogeneous segments whose members are more like each other than they are like the rest of the target population. The information provided by the market area analysis should offer some indication of potential market segments. In addition, the hospital may target, through other methods, special populations with which it wishes to establish a closer relationship.

Once these groups have been identified, an essential first step involves matching the provider's services and role with the specific target populations. To do this, the hospital must first describe in detail each targeted market segment of women it wishes to attract. Some market segments that have been found to be particularly responsive to specialized programs and services are:

- educated, upwardly mobile women having a first or second baby
- mothers of any age who deliver a malformed or dead infant
- mothers who prefer noninterventive, noninstitutional care
- professional women:
  — young, single
  — married with children
  — divorced with children
- post–childbearing age women dealing with life changes involving:
  — menopause
  — departure of children from home
  — re-entry into work force
  — loss of spouse
- older women:
  — married
  — divorced
  — widowed

> — chronically ill
> — primary caregivers
- women employees of the hospital
- physician office employees
- handicapped women

To decide how an individual program or service should be structured, each target population must be described in accordance with the list of differences among women given above. Once the market segments have been defined, the program can be developed with attention to the unique characteristics of each particular group. For example, if the hospital is developing an outpatient women's center and one targeted market segment is composed of divorced professional women with children, the following provisions should be included in program design:

- convenient hours of service:
  - early morning (before 8:00 A.M.)
  - evenings
  - weekends
- provisions for child care
- convenient location:
  - easy access
  - safe and well lighted
  - adequate parking
- sliding scale for payment
- special literature and counseling for single parents

Obviously, local differences warrant additions or variations and will influence program design in any particular community.

Which Programs To Develop

Once the market segments are identified, it will be necessary to avoid the urge to develop all possible programs and thus attempt to meet all of the needs of every target market segment. Simply because a need has been identified does not mean it is appropriate for the hospital to address it.

Decisions about new programs or services must be made with consideration given to the following:

- existing programs and services
- present organizational strengths
- role or mission of the hospital
- hospital's image with women in the community
- capabilities of the medical and nursing staff
- market niches filled or unfilled by competing health care providers
- financial ramifications
- intangible goodwill and market positioning
- degree of need and demand identified through the market area analysis
- regulatory issues

Careful market segmentation is necessary in order to provide a strong foundation for the other components of the marketing functions and process. In addition, well-developed market segmentation will provide a sound basis for volume projections and program usage.

Devising a Marketing Plan

Once the background data has been gathered and analyzed, target markets identified and described, and management's decisions communicated, the marketing program and action plan can be developed. If the hospital has chosen to form a marketing plan team or committee, its role in devising the plan can be one of the following:

1. Serve to develop the actual market plan document.
2. Review and comment on the document developed by other staff.

If the hospital does not wish to use a committee approach, development of the marketing program and action plan becomes a function for the marketing department and the caregiver management team of the program being developed.

If the hospital does not have a marketing department, a member of administration, in conjunction with the caregiver management team, can be assigned responsibility for developing the marketing program and action plan. Or, the hospital may wish to involve a consultant in plan activities in any of the above scenarios. The consultant's role will vary depending on the capabilities, sophistication, and time availability of the hospital staff.

Often, when many staff members are working jointly on a project, it is easy to overlook or fail to follow through on important details or commitments. In order to avoid this, the five following actions should be taken:

1. Establish measurable goals and objectives.
2. Assign specific duties or tasks to specific individuals.
3. Establish time frames for completion of duties and tasks.
4. Develop a process for monitoring the established schedules.
5. Allocate adequate time for staff involvement and completion of assigned responsibilities.

Establishment of Goals

Often, health care providers view goal setting as unnecessary or even a waste of time. Three reasons used to defend these attitudes are:

1. Everything is changing so fast that there is no point in establishing goals; new goals will have to be devised in a few months.
2. Feelings of impotence among staff, because the change occurs so fast, they think and feel they cannot control the outcomes.
3. It is much more important to do the work of implementing the programs than to sit around and write goals.

Staff members do not always seem to understand fully the role of or benefits of goal setting. Establishment of goals and objectives defines what is to be accomplished through the marketing activities. This process also provides a framework for evaluating the degree of success of the marketing effort.

For example, if the hospital is developing a new maternity care program, the following goals and objectives will be useful in defining and measuring program and marketing accomplishments:

- Increase patient volume by____percent during the next year.
- Capture ____percent of new patients from the areas identified as target markets.
- Attract and maintain new staff (nurses and obstetricians).
- Create a positive cash flow within the obstetrical service.

Identification of Provider Resources

The availability of resources sufficient to implement program development is crucial to the success of a project. Early in the marketing process, it will be necessary to evaluate existing and needed resources and to determine the action necessary to acquire resources currently unavailable.

With any new project, there is a tendency to think only in terms of people and dollars when resources are considered. The types and numbers of resources needed for program success encompass much more. They include:

- personnel
  - management and supervisory
  - physicians and nursing staff
  - ancillary and paramedical
  - clerical
- dollars
  - start-up funds
  - operating funds
- equipment
  - existing
  - new

- facility
  — space requirements (including expansion capabilities)
  — locations (in-house versus on-campus)
  — community-based
- political support
  — board
  — management
  — physician
  — community
- corporate or parent organization
- affiliated organizations

In evaluating and assessing resources, it is important to adopt a creative, expansive approach: Look beyond the obvious.

For example, one hospital was suddenly faced with the loss of its small obstetrics staff. At least two obstetricians were needed to build a foundation for recruiting additional physicians and rebuilding the obstetrical/gynecological service. The only other group of practicing obstetricians in the community was aligned with the hospital's competitor. These physicians were unwilling to provide obstetric care at two facilities or to admit patients to any but the competing hospital. Two other physicians primarily used the competing hospital, but occasionally delivered patients at the other hospital. One of these two physicians was the nephew of the former chairman of the board at the competing hospital. Because of this, it was assumed this young physician and his partner would be unwilling to accept a leadership role in reviving the service.

The authors came into the situation, as consultants often do, without the biases of the in-house staff. Noting the opportunity to attract these two physicians, it was suggested they be approached about the possibility of moving their practice to the hospital needing obstetricians. Management, although skeptical, was intrigued by the idea and gave the okay to meet with the doctors on their behalf. To management's surprise, the two doctors expressed significant interest in working with the hospital to provide the physician foundation needed to rebuild the service.

This is not an unusual occurrence. In fact, similar situations are common. The example is not provided with the intention of implying that the administration was not approaching resource identification in a thoughtful and searching manner. Rather, it is given to demonstrate how resource assessment and potential solutions are often obscured by past history and faulty or inadequate information.

Development of Promotion and Advertising

As noted earlier, promotion and advertising are generally the two components most visible in a marketing program. For many hospitals, these are the only components of the marketing process that are ever implemented. And, far too often, the implementation of these components is done in a fragmented or piecemeal way. To prevent this and avoid wasting allocated funds, it is recommended that the marketing process outlined in Chapter 1 be followed, and that a thoughtful, coordinated promotional and advertising campaign be developed *before* taking action.

Prior to embarking on a promotional or advertising campaign, it is necessary to determine the approach to be used and the desired image to be created. Image development must be done from the perspective of the target market. This may differ greatly from the image hospital staff believes should be conveyed or which is most pleasing to them. Information gathered through the market area analysis about the different target markets will be useful in making these distinctions.

Frequently, in an effort to move quickly and catch up, a hospital will embark on a promotional/advertising campaign by merely duplicating the promotional materials and media strategy of a competitor. The outcome of this marketing attempt can often cause the opposite effect from that which the hospital is seeking. Rather than distinguishing the hospital in its target markets, consumers will be given the impression that the facility is a follower, not a leader. This will only serve to reinforce and solidify the competitor's market position.

In this situation, professional help can be very effective. Public relations firms, advertising agencies, and marketing consultants with a knowledge and understanding of the women's market can assist with idea generation and strategy implementation. In order to attract patient interest, promotional and advertising campaigns must be unique and of high quality. Because of the limited experience health care providers have had in this area, most are unable to meet these standards by themselves. Yet, because of the cost, providers are often reluctant to spend the monies necessary to design and produce top-notch promotional and advertising campaigns. Often, the investment made in retaining professional assistance is offset by the benefits of a successful promotional and advertising campaign.

For maximum effectiveness, it is vital to maintain consistency and continuity in all events of the promotional and advertising campaign. This is accomplished through the use of a logo (representing the program); the same colors, print style, and appearance for all materials; and a common theme or slogan that appears in or on all materials. These campaign elements (including the theme or slogan) need to be attractive and appealing to women, especially the women identified in the target populations.

In some hospitals, the responsibility for developing promotional materials is given to nurses, community relations staff, education staff, or physicians. This is most commonly done when the motivation is to hold down costs by using in-house staff. Although the staff involved may have good intentions, many of them do not have the experience or the technical skills to produce the professional quality required.

For example, one hospital, hoping to keep expenses down, turned the production of a new brochure for a women's educational program over to an enthusiastic community relations coordinator. Chartreuse paper and bold black lettering were used. A tree with falling leaves had been chosen as the logo for the educational series of women's health care programs.

The young coordinator explained that she thought the bold color and lettering would be an effective way to attract interest for the program. To her, the tree symbolized the transition many women were experiencing in their lives. Her intentions were very good, but her knowledge and experience were too limited and caused her to make several questionable decisions.

She failed to recognize that unappealing colors attract attention, but not interest. Women might notice the chartreuse paper, but be unmotivated to take the time to read the brochure or even give it a second glance. What the tree represented to the young coordinator was too vague and ill-defined a symbol to be perceived consistently by women in her community. Some women might see the autumn tree as representative of transition in their lives, but the connection between the symbol and the idea of transition was not strong enough to convey the intended message to most women. Thus, this was not an effective way to promote the program. Objectives were not achieved, and both time and money were lost on the project.

In any promotional/advertising campaign, it is important to learn which methods for disseminating information are most effective in a facility's service area. Usually investigation will indicate that more than one method is desirable to effectively disseminate information to the public. Furthermore, the established advertising component of a hospital's marketing budget is rarely adequate to cover all possible advertising efforts. Thus, it will be necessary to prioritize the options based on predicted response and effectiveness. Here again, the results of the market area analysis will be helpful in prioritizing advertising efforts both before beginning a campaign and while the campaign is operational.

Once the campaign has been prepared, be certain to communicate all of the components to all hospital staff, including physicians. Not only is this an essential form of good public relations, but it also expands the flow of information transmitted to the community. The ramifications of not informing hospital staff and physicians can be harmful, for they will feel unimportant and left out. Consequently, many of them may be unwilling to support the program. Further, if asked about the program by family or friends, they will lack knowledge and may even feel animosity toward the program, thus negating some of the benefits of a promotional campaign.

Evaluation

One of the most commonly forgotten or neglected components of the marketing process is the evaluation component. Evaluation is an important way to find out how well the goals and objectives of the marketing plan have been met. Evaluation also provides up-to-date information on needed program modification and changes.

Methods for evaluation should be established prior to implementing the program. This will ensure compilation of the proper information to enable effective evaluation.

Patient response to services provides one of the most important means for evaluating program effectiveness. In today's client-driven market, the degree of patient satisfaction, with the service offered and with the manner in which it is delivered, frequently dictates the degree of success the program will have long-term.

Furthermore, women (and men) tend to form their opinion about the whole institution based upon their experience with one service. If this experience is good, they will have a positive image of the hospital. Not only will they use the hospital again, but they will also refer family and friends. Conversely, if the experience is negative, many women will assume all hospital services are questionable and communicate this negative message to anyone who will listen. Therefore, patient response becomes a good barometer for measuring the program and the hospital's reception in the community.

Methods for measuring patient satisfaction include:

- written questionnaires
- telephone interviews to assess satisfaction or to determine origins of dissatisfaction
- input from physicians regarding patients' reactions
- informal interviews by managers or supervisors with patients and visitors during the hospital stay
- suggestion boxes conveniently placed for patient or visitor use

In addition to patient response, other indicators of program success need to be monitored. Some relatively simple methods of evaluation are:

- Track the number of phone calls received in response to a new program or service.
- Repeat the public opinion section of the market area analysis to see how public perceptions or images have changed.

- Track the sources of information by which the public became aware of a new program or service.
- Track the changes in usage, by both patients and physicians, of existing programs.
- Track the changes in patient origin and market share for a new or existing program.
- Assess changes in morale and attitude among employees.

The overall marketing effort should be reviewed quarterly. New programs or services may need to be evaluated more frequently. In addition, all new programs should be evaluated within six weeks of implementation. This will identify program weaknesses early in the program and may prevent negative public reaction. Early evaluation will also allow corrections with staff, in procedure or methodology, before bad skills or habits have formed.

The evaluation component can be carried out by the marketing plan team or committee. If no committee exists, a hospital staff person, in top or middle management, can be given this responsibility. Here again, hospital administration may choose to hire an independent firm to conduct the evaluation. Regardless of who carries out the evaluation, results should be documented and reported to top management. Finally, timelines should be estimated and responsibility assigned for evaluation prior to program implementation. Creating this environment for the staff will facilitate quality and further ensure program success.

Chapter 3

Product Line Development

3

Product line is a term constantly bantered about. Yet rarely is it explained with clarity and frequently it is not understood. For the purposes of this book, it will be defined as follows.

> *Product line:* A single department or clinical service composed of multiple programs or products offered to the public.

Each individual clinical department in a hospital is an example of a product line. Such programs as childbirth education classes, antepartum testing, or home visits are individual products of the maternity service product line. An outpatient women's center is another product line. The products or services included in this product line are the education programs, screening and diagnostic services, counseling services, and the resource center.

Data from a market area analysis will identify both the product line and the products to be developed. Again, in making decisions from market area analysis data, it is important to clearly distinguish between interest for a product (service) to be offered and willingness to use the service.

Once the products for development have been identified, it is necessary to prioritize them for development. The tendency is to develop the product with the greatest indication of use from the respondents. That product, however, may not be the best choice.

Staff members involved in decision making must consider the availability of resources necessary for implementation. Sometimes
resources are readily available for the development of a product that
did not rank highest on the scale of willingness to use. However, if
the product is compatible with the goals and objectives of the overall
product line, and if enough support is indicated, development is
warranted. The hospital can benefit by moving forward with the
development of this less-than-highest-ranked product while mar-
shalling resources for the one ranked first.

For example, market area analysis information indicates strong,
positive response to the development of an outpatient women's
center (new product line). The service (product) that received the
strongest indication for potential usage was mammography. PMS
services (another product) were also ranked high for usage. To
establish mammography services, the hospital will need the latest
state-of-the-art equipment. It will take approximately six months to
receive the necessary approvals and purchase the equipment. But
one of the physicians on staff has already earned a reputation as a
PMS specialist. She is interested in opening a clinic in conjunction
with the hospital. The hospital can secure maximum return by
initiating the PMS program immediately, while staff move forward
with development of the mammography service.

Another consideration in product line development is to recognize and clearly define exactly what the customer is buying. For
example, when expectant parents come to a hospital for the birth of
their baby, they are not simply buying a safe delivery and hospital
stay. The couple are actually buying a fabulous experience in the life
of their family, not just labor, delivery, and postpartum care. Good
care is expected and taken as a given. Beyond this, they wish to have
all of the amenities of family-centered maternity care, and provision
of these may be the deciding factor in their selection of a hospital.

During the course of product line development, significant benefit
can be derived by adopting the well-known concept of the *add-on
sale*. The add-on sale is the art of turning one sale into many. For
example, a pregnant patient calls the hospital to register for the
childbirth education classes. The hospital offers four other classes
for expectant parents. The hospital staff member, who understands
the add-on sales concept, will use this opportunity to make the

patient aware of these additional classes. The staff member will also get the patient's name and address for future mailings in addition to sending the patient a brochure describing the expectant parents classes.

This same concept should be used when developing product lines. One product often generates the need for other products. For example, if an outpatient women's center is opened, with several products (services) available to women, a need for childcare often arises. Providing that care, as part of the the women's center, constitutes the development of an additional product (service) and expansion of the product line (see Figure 3–1).

CREATING THE PRODUCT

From the market area analysis, potential product lines and individual products are identified and prioritized based on consumer preference, competitive assessment, and management approval.

In accordance with these decisions, operational and financial feasibility is assessed for each product line or product (see Figure 3–2). From this analysis, those projects with the greatest potential for immediate implementation and return are identified. Product lines or products that do not appear feasible are abandoned or returned to the options list for re-evaluation at a later date.

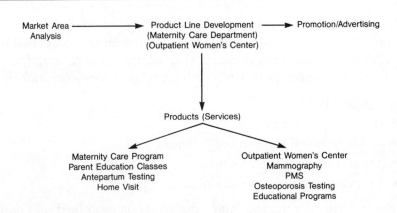

Figure 3–1 Product Line Development

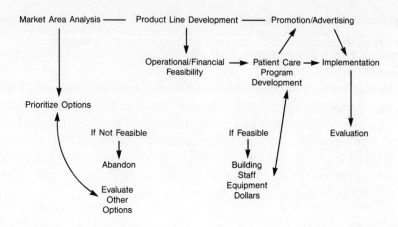

Figure 3–2 Flow Chart for Feasibility Analysis

An operational-financial feasibility study can be divided into five major areas of activity:

1. the cataloging of potential services that can be offered
2. the development of potential service base combinations
3. the projection of service volume
4. the determination of necessary resources
5. the projection of financial commitment

In order to illustrate the process, we will use the following example. A hospital has decided to develop an outpatient women's center as a new product line. One of the products to be offered will be a program for osteoporosis testing and diagnosis. Project responsibility has been assigned to the coordinator of the women's center. She has formed a committee to assist with the project. Members include:

- a gynecologist
- an exercise therapist
- an RN who will work in the program
- a representative from finance
- a representative from marketing.

The five areas of the feasibility study can be examined and data gathered by the committee under the leadership of the coordinator.

When conducting an operational-financial feasibility study, it is important to begin by listing all of the potential program components that can be offered. This list needs to be all-inclusive, for it will serve as a catalog from which the hospital will select those program components it chooses to offer. The list for osteoporosis screening will look like this:

- osteoporosis screening
  —dual photon
  —treatment
  —research projects
  —exercise programs
  —educational programs
  —nutritional counseling

The second step is to use the catalog to develop service base combinations. It is suggested that several possible service combinations be considered to guide the feasibility assessment process.

Projections of volume will need to be developed for each service offered within each of the possible combinations that are under consideration. Volume projections can be based on findings from the market area analysis. Information from similar programs developed in other parts of the country will also be useful in projecting volume, assuming patient mix and other demographics are similar.

Volume projections are generally done for a three year time period (monthly for the first year, annually thereafter). However, because of the rapidly changing health care environment, the committee may wish to make projections of volume for a shorter period. In either case, volume projections must be reviewed and revised regularly. With new programs, it is preferable to review and make revisions on a monthly basis for the first year, followed by quarterly review and revision thereafter.

Once all of the resources needed for each combination of services have been identified, projections of financial commitment for each combination can be done. Expenses need to be organized into three categories:

- start-up costs
- capital expenses
- operating costs

As with volume projections, operating expense projections must be done on a monthly basis for the first year. Once the program is established, the projections can be done annually.

Before making a final selection from the service base combinations, a number of other factors need to be considered. They are:

1. physician acceptance and support
2. regulatory and licensing issues
3. timeline for implementation
4. affiliation or joint venture possibilities
5. community acceptance
6. promotional advantage and market position potential
7. liability

At the conclusion of the operational-financial feasibility study, a choice must be made among the service base combinations. This selection will be based upon the hospital's purpose or rationale for initiating a particular new product. Some typical selection criteria are:

- return on investment
- retention of existing patients
- attraction of new patients
- image enhancement
- compatibility with existing services and programs
- solidification of market position
- uniqueness in the market place
- availability of physician expertise

Once the product has been selected from the service base combinations and the necessary approval has been given for implementation, the patient care program can now be developed. Development of the patient care program is the clinical aspect of product development. Some of the components to be developed at this stage are:

- a statement of philosophy
- clinical policies and procedures
- treatment protocols
- research protocols (if applicable)
- forms and information documents
- reimbursement procedures
- staffing requirements

PROMOTIONAL PLAN FORMATION

A promotional plan outlines the sequential staging of the special events and advertising that create visibility for and attract attention to a new or refined product. A promotional plan includes:

- a schedule for the type of media to be used
- a schedule of special events
- the timelines for completion of individual tasks
- the preparation of printed materials

The primary purpose of a promotional/advertising plan is to ensure that the product receives ongoing, positive attention and the visibility necessary to attract new patients. The promotional plan is developed after the patient care program has been established, and it is often done during the implementation phase. Promotional plans are frequently coordinated by the marketing department or other staff members overseeing the marketing plan.

One of the first issues that always surfaces when developing a marketing/promotional/advertising plan is the dilemma associated with budget formation. Frequently no monies have been designated for promotion and advertising. Herein lies the dilemma: Because there is no established budget, a conflict exists regarding how to arrive at the dollar amount to be budgeted. Marketing staff want to know how much they can spend before they decide what can be done. Management staff want to know how much can be done, before deciding what to spend.

In order to formulate the most creative and effective plan possible, the promotional plan should be developed before the budget is established. This will bring to the table the plan that best presents the product. If the proposed plan requires a budget exceeding the amount management is willing to allocate, individual parts may be eliminated, leaving a sound program with which to work.

One factor that may limit the content of the plan is the time available before product initiation. The number and complexity of the promotional/advertising activities need to be tailored to match the time available. There is real danger in this. If the timeline is too short, it may not be possible to conduct a promotional program that achieves the desired results.

A second consideration in establishing timelines involves staging. For maximum impact, promotional and advertising programs need to be spread over a period of time. Often enthusiasm and inexperience cause hospital staff to clump together all activities in an entire program at product initiation. Certainly, that is a crucial time to focus a major portion of the promotional/advertising/campaign resources. However, in order to maintain the visibility established at program initiation, some of the activities need to be reserved for later use. If the events are not staged periodically, ongoing visibility, which is the purpose of the plan, is not achieved.

The intent of a promotional/advertising program is to create or enhance an image. In order to do so, the hospital must define this image before the promotional/advertising plan is developed. Once the image has been defined, it will help guide not only the promotional/advertising program, but also all other facets of the product design.

Because so much is riding on the promotional/advertising plan, it may be cost-effective to involve outside consultants in plan development. This is particularly useful when the following conditions exist:

1. A promotional/advertising program that is large and complex in scope is to be executed.
2. The hospital has:

- a small, already overburdened marketing staff
- an inexperienced marketing staff
- no marketing staff.

3. The competition has a highly sophisticated marketing program.
4. The time frames for development and execution are short.
5. Special knowledge of the particular market or product line is not available in-house.

IMPLEMENTATION OF THE PRODUCT

For many people, implementation seems to mean the final stage of product development—opening the door and providing the service. But in fact, implementation involves completing and coordinating all of the activities that are part of product line development.

In order to ensure a successful outcome, implementation must be carried out in an orderly fashion. It will be necessary to adjust the schedules and responsibilities of staff members who are involved in carrying out the development/implementation process. Often this is not done. Because hospitals are forced to extract increased productivity from a smaller number of staff members, it is difficult to justify or even consider the removal or reduction of everyday responsibilities for those staff given the task of developing a new product. However, to ensure adequate and appropriate decision making and performance, both with respect to the new program and to everyday responsibilities, adjustment of schedules and duties must be made.

The establishment of timelines and accountability throughout the development/implementation process is essential. These controls will work to keep the entire process moving forward in a timely manner.

MONITORING RESULTS

It was mentioned earlier that evaluation was the most often forgotten component in the marketing process. In addition to its being often forgotten, there are two negative attitudes frequently associated with evaluation, in particular, with the process of checking and verifying results.

First, after working feverishly to develop and implement a product, staff tend to think the job is done. Thus, conducting an evaluation or monitoring function is perceived as a nuisance and of no real benefit to the program. Staff members with this attitude think evaluation is a burden, to be done only if required. The second attitude views evaluation as a "nice thing to do if there is time," but not really necessary for program success. A staff member with this attitude fails to recognize the importance of evaluation and is unlikely to ever give any time to the evaluation process.

Frequently program staff fail to consider the evaluation process until after the program is operational. In these instances, staff often find that the data required for evaluation have not been collected. An evaluation plan needs to be developed before a program begins functioning. This will ensure that a mechanism is designed to secure the data necessary to conduct thorough and proper program evaluation.

Evaluation is arguably no less important than any other component in the marketing process. In order to ensure that evaluation is conducted regularly, top management must require completion of this final step in the product development process and support the allocation of resources needed to accomplish it. In the case of a women's center or maternity care unit, the program coordinator can be responsible for establishing the evaluation and monitoring component and reporting the findings to top management.

RESPONDING TO RESULTS

In the course of program evaluation, problems will be uncovered. Most often these problems involve how patients responded to care received. For this reason, a two-pronged approach is most effective in handling the results of the evaluation process. One facet of the approach involves solving or removing the problem. The other aspect of this approach focuses on eliminating or resolving bad feelings among the patients.

Reducing Negative Feelings

As often noted, the patient's perception of a hospital is shaped by her own experiences (regardless of how limited) and by the opinions of others. If what the patient experiences and what she hears are positive, she will be willing to use the hospital again and to recommend it to others. Conversely, if the patient has a negative encounter, she will be reluctant or even unwilling to come back or to advise her family and friends to use the hospital. Thus, every negative patient response has powerful ramifications. These responses must not be dismissed as insignificant.

Certainly, some patient dissatisfaction occurs with even the most effective programs. Thus, in every program significant effort must be expended to eliminate conditions that generate negative responses. But simply solving the problems that cause patient dissatisfaction is not enough. An equally intense effort must be directed to resolving negative outcomes once they have occurred. Eliminating problems may reduce concerns for future users, yet it does not alter the negative feelings of previous patients. Only evidence that the hospital cares about the patients' reaction can achieve this result.

There are a number of ways that hospital staff can demonstrate they care. Telephone calls and letters are an effective means for telling patients that their feedback has been heard and that action has been taken. Communication carries more weight with a patient if it comes from supervisory staff. The patient then feels that not only did the hospital hear and give validity to the complaint, but also someone in a position of authority is attending to the situation. A follow-up letter or call explaining the action taken and thanking the patient for the feedback is an excellent way to reinforce how important the patient is to the hospital.

Sometimes the situation that caused patient dissatisfaction cannot be easily or quickly corrected. In these instances, it is still very important to respond promptly to a patient's feedback. For example, some hospitals have added a few special birthing rooms to their traditional maternity care services. As the availability of these birthing rooms becomes known, utilization increases. Some patients planning to use a birthing room may arrive in labor only to find that none are available. When this situation occurs, there is usually disappointment and resentment, for the patient will not have the type of birth experience anticipated.

Certainly, over time the hospital can create more birthing room suites to avoid this occurrence in the future. But the addition of more rooms does not address the disappointment the woman and her family felt when what they were "promised" was not available. However, the hospital can show that it understands the family's feelings of disappointment. A bouquet of flowers accompanied by a note acknowledging the situation will help offset any negative feelings the family may have about the hospital.

In fact, gestures like this can turn a potentially bad experience into a positive one. Most patients are very favorably impressed by the personal attention their problems receive. They interpret this to mean that the hospital does care about them as individuals. The tendency is to assume that a given problem was an unusual event and not the normal occurrence at the hospital. It allows a patient to have a positive image of the hospital, even though her personal experience was not totally satisfactory.

Eliminating Problems

Although solving a problem causing patient dissatisfaction clearly is not the only kind of action required, it surely is an important one. Patient response can be an important tool in identifying problem areas. However, it rarely provides enough information to fully define the problem. If problems are to be resolved, staff must conduct further research to determine what must be done and how change can be accomplished, quickly and effectively.

In many hospitals the organizational structure does not accommodate this kind of problem solving. Frequently problems in one department cause negative feelings about another department or service. For example, if a woman in labor must wait to be admitted or must be separated from her husband while he completes admission forms and provides financial information, she may well have negative feelings about the hospital's maternity care program. She will enter the maternity care unit already angry and frustrated, creating a tense situation which the staff must now work to resolve. However, the usual chain of command does not allow the obstetric program manager the opportunity to research and correct problems in the admitting department.

Often, the creation of a patient representative or administrative assistant will help to offset these difficulties. Persons in such positions can investigate problems that cross department lines, convene interdisciplinary task forces to study them, and make recommendations to the appropriate managers for problem resolution. These individuals can also establish contact with patients while they are hospitalized to address concerns before they become major problems and follow-up on patient problems that surface after discharge.

In conclusion, evaluation without follow-up is empty. Responding to the results of the evaluation process is an essential step in assuring program effectiveness. To fully resolve the problems identified, the response must deal not only with correcting the problem, but also with addressing the feelings patients have about their experience. Since the patient's perception is reality, no problem can be truly resolved until the patient's feelings have been made whole.

Part II

Innovative Women's Services: The Reproductive Years

Chapter 4

What Expectant Parents Want

4

Issues present in the health care industry of the mid-1980s have catapulted maternity services into a priority position for marketability review and evaluation. The assertive, sometimes rebellious, childbearing age woman has come head to head with traditional obstetrical practices. Added to this is the impact women have on the health care marketplace, the competition among health care providers, plummeting utilization of hospital beds, and frantic efforts, both internal and external, to control costs. All of these issues have stimulated renewed interest in maternity programs and forced administration to take a fresh look at their capabilities to respond to the contemporary health care environment.

The utilization of marketing strategies and principles is essential as program changes are planned and implemented. Essential questions must be answered:

- Does the provider know what services patients desire for their childbearing experience?
- Does the program provide the components or amenities today's obstetrical patient is seeking?
- How do area maternity services compare regarding cost, program options, public perception?
- What is needed to move this program into a premier position in the eyes of the public it serves?

Determining the answers to these questions is a critical first step in learning what patients want and need for a pleasing childbirth experience.

Currently, an average of 1.7 children are born to each family in the United States.[1] Childbirth is one of the most significant events that occurs during a family's lifetime. Because most couples are having only one or two children, they do not have multiple chances to "get it right." They are reading scores of articles and books about innovative, meaningful childbirth experiences. Today's parents are shopping for that special program that will include them as partners in the health care team, allowing them to make informed choices about their birth event. People do not just buy things, they buy expectations. One such expectation is that what is purchased will produce the benefits promised.[2] Thus, the hospital that truly provides family-centered maternity care will emerge as the preferred choice of today's expectant parents.

Data from national surveys conducted by market consultants and market researchers indicate that catering to the maternity market segment is critical to patient acquisition, not only for the maternity department, but for other health services as well. Thirty-eight percent of maternity clients have their first experience with a hospital through their initial birth event. This point of entry into the health care system for a young family offers tremendous marketing potential. A positive experience with a well-planned and implemented family-oriented maternity program can cement a long-term relationship with the hospital, encouraging the family to return again and again, for other health care needs.

Another statistic providing impetus to hospitals to upgrade maternity care services is that sixty-seven percent of all health care decisions are made by women. Not only do they direct their own care, but they influence family and friends regarding where, how, and when health care is sought. Considering these two statistics alone, it is not difficult to understand the far-reaching ramifications, both positive and negative, for future patient acquisition and changing market share.

HAVING THE RIGHT PRODUCT

Often the first direct contact a potential patient has with the maternity program is a visit to the unit. Many women "drop in" to see the unit and ask questions about the program, specific to their needs. Others participate in routine tours conducted by unit staff, often in connection with prenatal classes. Market surveys indicate that women today will shop for the program they desire, inquiring into an average of three facilities.

When touring or visiting a maternity unit, according to these same surveys, a woman will make a decision within approximately four minutes as to whether or not she is interested in having her baby at that hospital. Interestingly, she will base much of this decision on the appearance and cleanliness of the unit and the friendliness of the staff. Although these are not the only program elements for which she is shopping, her first impression of the unit and the manner in which she is treated by the nursing staff will directly affect her decision to proceed with questions about the program.

Health care personnel are often dismayed that women will base utilization decisions on such "trivial" issues. "What about competency and technology?" they ask. In discussion, women state that they cannot judge competency from their perspective, and furthermore, they expect it from the health care provider. Technology and competency tend to be assessed on the basis of appearance, both of the physical plant and the staff. In fact, this manner of assessment is no different than that used by consumers walking into a business or a hotel lobby. Everyone tends to make assessments of competency and state-of-the-art technology based on the condition and appearance of the equipment and physical plant. Everyone judges service by the friendliness and attention paid by the staff—in a hospital, a hotel, or a business office.

If the decor and physical aspects of the maternity care unit look old, outdated, and unclean, the patient assumes that the latest care methods and techniques will not be provided. This assumption is particularly significant, since few hospitals have invested in the obstetrical program and structural improvements in recent years. Many facilities today look like they did in the 1950s: old, tired, cluttered, unattractive and institutional, thereby suggesting technological obsolescence.

To ensure a positive first impression and increase the possibility of capturing the shopping maternity patient, careful attention must be given to decor and physical remodeling. The public entrance to the unit should be designed as an inviting focal point. Interior decoration and furnishings of the entire unit must be warm and comfortable, with soft, relaxing colors that are attractive to women. Carpeting, wallpaper, and upholstered furniture create a calm, quiet, homelike atmosphere.

Internal marketing programs, often called guest-relations or customer relations programs, help staff members learn the importance and techniques of greeting the public positively. The goal is to treat patients and their families—and potential patients and the general public as well—as honored guests at all times. Women clearly indicate the importance of this when relating their experiences with health care staff. Often what seemed to be a minor incident will color, positively or negatively, the patient's feelings about the hospital and program. Being too busy to smile, say hello, or answer a question or two does not make the patient or family member think the staff member is important and hardworking. Quite the contrary, most people respond to a "too busy" reaction by assuming that the hospital is understaffed, disorganized, and inefficient. Again, using an example from another industry, how does one feel when one walks into a hotel lobby and all of the employees are "too busy" to say hello or answer a question about directions? Or another example: If a patient in labor is greeted by a thoughtless comment such as "Oh no, not another admission! We will never get dinner tonight," both the patient and her family will feel anger, disappointment, and concern about their choice of hospital. The staff member who takes the time to warmly greet anyone appearing at the nurses' station inquiring about the program, or being admitted, makes that person feel important and respected.

Physical appearance, decor, and positive staff attitudes, while very important, are meaningless without a program to market once the patient is interested. Putting a pretty wrapping around the same old package and claiming it is new will induce resentment in the well-read woman seeking a special birth event. Likewise, the staff will become frustrated and disillusioned with the responsibility of promoting a positive environment when old rules obstruct the provision of options that families perceive as available.

FAMILY-CENTERED MATERNITY CARE

What exactly is family-centered maternity care? Wallpaper and flowers, a champagne dinner, or a service-oriented staff? Almost every hospital that provides maternity care today claims to have family-centered maternity care, but only a few seem to know how to really provide it.

Family-centered maternity care, by its broadest definition, provides the birth environment parents today are seeking. We define family-centered maternity care not as a program element, but as an attitude and philosophy about birth. It is care which treats childbirth as a once-in-a-lifetime family celebration. Often health care providers, who deliver six thousand or three thousand or even seven hundred babies a year, forget how important childbirth is to the family. It is important to remember, that even though the hospital delivered three thousand babies this year, the parents are having only one baby all year long, and it is a very big deal!

This wonderful event belongs to the family, to be experienced in ways that make it meaningful to them. They allow hospital employees and physicians the privilege of participating in this special time because of the medical backup and expertise needed for the safety of mother and newborn. This philosophical approach, together with a warm, friendly, attractive, nonchaotic environment, brings the program to life for the shopping consumer.

OPTIONS, OPTIONS, OPTIONS

To effectively change to a market-sensitive maternity program, it is critical to look carefully at the many options expectant parents of today are seeking. It must be recognized that the family-centered philosophy and attitudes supportive of desired options are often in direct conflict with the restrictive rules, policies, and care methods still considered to be "sacred" in traditional obstetrics. Often the staff, unconsciously resisting change, will develop multiple arguments as to why care will be compromised if the old way of doing things is changed. Hospital management, together with nursing and physician leaders, must challenge these arguments by asking the following questions:

1. Why can't we change? What is really keeping us from changing?
2. What are the objective data that substantiate the argument?
3. Whose needs are most important, the patients' or the staff's?

Working through these questions will help both management and staff achieve the mind-shift necessary to make meeting patients' needs a simple reality.

Following are some components and options of family-centered maternity programs that market research shows are important to contemporary maternity patients. It should be noted that the options described below are most often requested by educated, sophisticated, private-paying patients, among others.

Partner Participation

The shared participation of patient and partner in the childbirth experience, where fathers are encouraged, not merely allowed, to share the experiences, has become an important aspect of maternity care.

The crescendo of consumerism in recent years and its effect on changing the delivery of maternity care started in part with the demand that fathers be allowed in the delivery room for the birth of the infant. From this beginning point, expectant couples have continued to pressure physicians, hospital staff, and other maternity providers to personalize the birth experience. They want the option of participating together through the entire birth process: pregnancy, labor, delivery, and parenting of the newborn. Attending prenatal education classes together, with involvement of the father in prenatal physician visits when possible, promotes a supportive and understanding relationship regarding the effects of pregnancy and the birth process. Sharing in the care of the newborn while still in the hospital helps both parents become better acquainted with their infant and develop the emotional bonds of a new family unit.

Decision-Making Involvement

Parents seek inclusion and involvement as participants in the decision-making process. They want to be encouraged, through the sharing of information pertinent to their specific situation, to make informed decisions about their birth event.

Again, it must be stressed that birth is a family event. Members of the health care team should facilitate the experience, not dominate it. Many physicians and nurses are fearful of losing control if they allow patients and their partners a voice in the decisions being made during the hospital stay. Loss of control in fact has not materialized when the involvement is supported by the health care provider in an open and genuine manner. To the contrary, the pregnant patient and her partner are often less confrontive and demanding when they are encouraged to express their needs, included in all decisions about the status and progress of the pregnancy, and helped to make quality decisions based on full knowledge of the implications of the decision options.

Viewing birth as a normal family process shifts the focus of childbirth from a medical or surgical crisis to a meaningful, satisfying experience for the maternity patient and her family. The nurse, physician, and family, working closely together, become a team in which informed consent is an ongoing process throughout the childbearing process.

Inclusion of Family and Friends

Couples often desire to involve significant family members, including brothers and sisters of the newborn, as well as support persons. They encourage family and friends to see and talk with the patient during labor, to attend the birth, and to visit the postpartum patient.

It is important for maternity care personnel to be sensitive to the needs and desires of each mother in labor. This sensitivity requires that the health care worker not allow his or her values to interfere or overrule the values of the mother or father.

People celebrate in different ways: some quietly, one-on-one, and some with gusto, involving family and friends. As long as the safety of the mother during labor and the newborn is not compromised, the parents should decide who is present for their child's birth. This is a very individualized decision and should be made by the parents—together with the physician if the hospital has a policy supporting this option.

The advisability of children attending the birth of their new sibling is still being debated in many circles. Parents who feel strongly that their children be present must plan for the event with the physician and the hospital or facility staff. Sibling education and preparation are usually required and beneficial. A support person must be present for each child planning to attend the birth. It is the specific responsibility of that support person to accompany the child, answer questions, and observe the child for untoward reactions. The support person is expected to leave the mother's room with the child if negative reactions develop. Once birth has occurred, the sibling may return to the family gathering to share the experience of the emerging new family unit.

Postpartum Contact

Many parents have come to expect immediate and prolonged contact with the newborn following birth and the promotion of family bonding in a private, nurturing, safe environment.

Another target of today's assertive maternity consumers is elimination of the traditional practice of whisking the newborn away to isolation in the nursery immediately after birth. These consumers, motivated to optimal childbirth outcomes for their newborn and the family unit, are reading articles and books expounding the values of early parent/infant contact. They will search for a physician and a childbearing facility that are sensitive to and promote these values.

Studies on parent/infant attachment and bonding support early contact between parents and newborn. Intense parent-to-infant attraction usually occurs as a rapid process following birth.[3] In addition, it has been shown that the newborn infant is alert during the first hour or two after birth and has the ability to discriminate among various stimuli, including recognition of the voices of the mother and father, which were heard in utero.

Further indication for mother and baby to be together during the first three to four hours following delivery has been provided by Dr. Marshall Klaus. In studies conducted at the State University, Michigan, Dr. Klaus found that just after delivery the mother's receptivity to learning is greatly enhanced. Having the baby with her during these first three to four hours provides an excellent opportunity for the perinatal nurse to give information and assistance to the mother and father along with early care and support.[4]

At first reluctantly, but more recently wholeheartedly, physicians and hospitals have slowly acceded to patient demands for changes in the practice of nursery observation.[5] Several decades ago, as fetal/infant physiological changes at birth were becoming better understood, the medical community was overwhelmed by the potential for complications. Close observation of newborns was mandated for the first twenty-four hours after birth. However, evaluation of the incidence of complications indicates that the routine isolation and monitoring as it has been practiced is seldom necessary.

Changes in obstetrical practices that favorably affect outcomes for both mother and infant justify relaxation of policies dictating mandatory nursery observation unless complications arise. The ill effects of excessive sedation and analgesia on mother or infant are not as common a problem given the increase of more natural childbirth experiences.

Effective, safe observation and care of the newborn can occur in the childbearing room immediately following birth, while supporting parent/infant bonding and attachment. This has been demonstrated by hospitals across the country for several years. The change in thinking by the medical and nursing staff in these programs is to expect a normal childbirth outcome, rather than a potential medical emergency. The assessment skills of the nurse and physician in attendance ensure that if infant complications occur, they are rapidly identified and resolved. When the parents have been actively involved in the birth process, they understand and accept separation from their infant when it is necessary for an identified problem. They do not understand or accept separation from their infant when it is done merely because of "hospital policy."

Availability of Rooming-In

Parents want the opportunity to have the infant in the family's hospital room twenty-four hours per day. Mothers want the availability of twenty-four hour rooming-in. Some wish to have the infant in their room at all times, some only for certain hours of the day and the evening. The important issue is that they want the privilege or option of deciding, at any point in time during the postpartum stay, when they want to have their baby with them.

This change in practice, the promotion of unlimited rooming-in, has been difficult for many physicians and nurses to accept. Mothers state that they often feel as if they are in a tug-of-war with the hospital staff. They request the infant be kept in their room, but the nurses keep taking him or her back to the nursery for routine vital sign checks, infant care, or doctor's examinations. Most mothers want infant care done in their rooms, so they can participate and learn about the baby.

Hospital staff members express fear and concern about allowing a newborn to stay in the mother's room during the night. Many new mothers tell us their concerns about hearing the baby or caring for it at night, and want to "practice," keeping the baby in the room at night, with ample help nearby, before going home.

Careful, ongoing nursing assessment of the status of both mother and infant is integral to safe, twenty-four hour rooming-in. Under normal conditions, a mother will easily be awakened by the sounds of her infant. However, if she is unusually exhausted or receiving medication for sleep, her response to the infant will predictably be altered. In such cases, it is not appropriate to leave the infant in the childbearing room. Likewise, if the infant is exhibiting any symptoms requiring close observation, such as excessive mucus, he or she is better cared for in the nursery, while the mother is sleeping. In either case, objective data need to be discussed with the mother, helping her understand the need for deviation from her wishes for twenty-four hour rooming-in.

Reduced Medical Intervention

Patients tend to prefer limited medical intervention unless specific medical needs are present. This calls for retraining the medical and nursing staff in the use of "routine" care to allow the patient in labor more choices and more time.

Consumer rebellion against traditional obstetrical practice focuses in part on the belief that much medical intervention is unnecessary and interferes with the desired celebration of childbirth as a normal family event. This belief, championed by maternity consumer advocacy groups, was a significant factor in the increased incidence of home births over the past years. Women are emphatically saying they will not accept the routine use of perineum shaves, enemas, intravenous fluids, electronic devices, sterile rooms, and bright surgical lights.

Preference profiles, birth plans, and birth contracts prepared by expectant parents have evolved to express this demand for change. When presented, they should be viewed as positive, practical tools for communication between health care providers and family members.[6] In fact, many physicians who are attuned to the market are suggesting prenatally to expectant parents that they discuss and prepare in writing a birth plan identifying their specific needs and desires. The physician can then sit down with the mother and father and review the stated plan in preparation for the birth.

Sometimes, birth plan requests must be negotiated. One request frequently included on a birth plan is "no fetal monitoring." No physician, especially in today's litigious society, will agree to this request without qualification. But in the quiet atmosphere of the physician's office at a prenatal visit, the plan can be discussed openly and a compromise plan of action agreed upon.

Unfortunately, such negotiation occurs more frequently after the patient has been admitted in labor. This is not the best time or place for negotiation to occur. The physician often feels compromised and the parents feel cheated or betrayed. The more discussions of parents' needs and wishes that occur prenatally, the clearer will be everyone's expectations and understanding at the time of labor and delivery.

If birth plan requests are not in conflict with hospital or nursing practices, discussion with hospital staff prior to admission is usually not required. However, the physician should bring hospital staff into prenatal plan discussions when hospital issues also need to be negotiated. In either instance, the birth plan, whether formal or merely a collection of documented notes, should be sent to the hospital with the prenatal record prior to the labor admission. Effective communication, between health care providers and parents, demonstrates to the family that their needs and wishes are important.

Helping the family understand and accept medical intervention when needed on an individual basis is the key to a satisfactory outcome. Sharing information with the patient and her partner during the childbirth process facilitates reasonable and effective decision making.

Visiting Privileges

Mothers want unrestricted visiting privileges, including twenty-four hour sleeping accommodations, for the husband or partner. Fathers want the option to stay at the hospital and participate in the care of the baby.

As with rooming-in, women are very vocal about the option to decide how much or how little their husband or partner stays with them in the hospital. Work patterns and life styles vary greatly from couple to couple. Unrestricted visiting privileges for the father allow parents total flexibility for family time together in the hospital, whenever they wish, day or night, and to balance such times with the partner's other needs and work schedule. Guest trays and beverages should also be provided, free of hassle and with a smile.

The option for husband or partner to sleep in the mother's room is a much sought after feature by many of today's obstetrical consumers. Some maternity care facilities offer double beds for parents who wish to use them. Most programs, however, provide a slumber chair or sleeper couch that can be opened into a single bed for the husband or partner. Feedback from couples indicates that sharing the experience by sleeping in the same room is important, not necessarily sleeping in the same bed.

This program feature may cause value conflicts for nurses and physicians. Health care staff sometimes express great discomfort with this practice. Many feel it is inappropriate and fear they will be expected to monitor sexual activity. Togetherness, embracing, and cuddling with the baby or each other are expressions of love and affection to be encouraged at this time of family celebration. The incidence of sexual intercourse resulting from this option has not been shown to be any greater than that occurring in traditional maternity programs.

In this and all aspects of an option-oriented, family-centered obstetrics program, health care staff must continually assess their personal attitudes, beliefs, and values. Patients and their families are influenced positively or negatively in every contact with a health care provider. Research has shown that in a hospital of one hundred beds, approximately 25,000 interactions between staff and patients or family occur daily. Staff attitudes and behavior will color each of these encounters.[7]

Value conflicts related to options for patients must be recognized and discussed among the staff. Consumers expect the hospital to provide a safe and appropriate environment to meet their needs, not mandate personal values that may differ from their own.

Family Visiting Privileges

Parents often desire liberal, if not unrestricted, visiting privileges for the grandparents and brothers and sisters of the newborn, including support for these special visitors to see and hold the new baby in the mother's room.

Most expectant couples wish their parents and other children to be active participants in the childbirth event. Parents may or may not wish them to be present at the birth, but having them visit and be in physical contact with the newborn is of paramount importance.

A new family unit is created with the addition of a baby. The bonding and attachment process, although most critical for the parents and infant, involves the entire immediate family. Grandparents and siblings need time with the parents and infant to be encouraged to hold the new baby and even participate in early care of both mother and infant. Observations of families and feedback from them indicate that sibling jealousy is reduced when the children share actively in the interactions around the childbirth experience.[8] Also, visitation of siblings with their mother helps them react much more positively to the separation caused by the hospitalization.[9]

Liberal visiting times, for the grandparents and siblings, are important for the same reasons stated for the father. A family member's work, school, or other activities should not need alteration to adapt to a restrictive sibling and grandparent visitation policy.[10]

An often heard concern is that liberalized visiting privileges will open a floodgate and be abused. In practice, this does not occur. When allowed the freedom to come and go according to their needs, family members are reasonable and sensible. Abuses, when they do occur, can be dealt with on an individual basis.

Mother/Baby Nursing

Nursing care provided to mother and newborn as a family unit by the same nurse promotes and supports development of a relationship between the mother and nurse. This creates a link tying the family to the hospital.

When given the choice, women prefer a system of nursing assignment called mother/baby nursing. In this system, nurses on each shift are assigned the care of mothers and infants as family units. This is in contrast to the traditional method of assignment in which the care involves at least two nurses, one providing postpartum care for the mother and one providing nursery care for the infant. Two common complaints often heard about traditional staffing patterns are:

- One asks the postpartum nurse a question about the infant and is told the nursery nurse must provide the answer.
- One gets a different or conflicting answer to the same question from each nurse providing care.

With mother/baby nursing, since only one nurse is responsible for both mother and infant, the care activities for both are carried out, as much as possible, in the mother's room. Care and teaching are provided to mother and infant together. As a result, fragmentation is diminished and the continuity of care and quality of teaching are much improved. Nurses become more involved with family members and a strong bond develops. Mothers verbalize that they feel as if they are getting more care and attention from the nursing staff than in traditional systems. A side benefit to hospitals is the cost effectiveness and staff satisfaction derived from this staffing pattern.

In-Room Examinations

Parents benefit from examination of the newborn in the mother's room by the pediatrician or family physician. This increases the learning opportunities for the parents by encouraging greater participation.

Mothers express strong feelings when asked if they would like the physician to examine their baby in their room. They want to be involved, observe the examination, and be able to ask questions about the baby. Frustration and anger are expressed with the traditional practice of the physician examining the infant in the nursery and reporting results to the mother. Mothers state that they often forget to ask questions of the physician and generally feel dissatisfied with the exchange of information.

The physician who goes one step further and invites the mother, whose infant cannot be in her room because of complications, to come to the nursery to observe the examination, is held in high regard. Sensitive pediatricians and family physicians across the country are learning the positive benefits to this change in hospital infant care. Parents learn more and develop greater loyalty to their doctor. Physicians who provide such care will reap the benefits of a busy and successful practice.

Educational Programs

It is important to increase educational programs and teaching throughout the pregnancy, childbirth, and postpartum periods, providing parents with more knowledge and hospitals with more satisfied patients.

The thirst for knowledge in today's health care consumer is well recognized. Interest in wellness, disease prevention, and greater self-care has increased among people of all ages, especially women. Women demonstrate much greater interest in health care information about themselves and their families than in the past.

Families desire a broad range of education and knowledge about the entire childbearing experience. Comprehensive maternity care programs include a wide variety of perinatal care options, such as classes in nutrition, self-image, sibling preparation, grandparenting,

parenting for fathers, parenting for teenagers, grieving parents and prenatal and postnatal exercises.

Private Rooms

Women desire private hospital rooms to promote the attachment process for the new family unit. Privacy and the accompanying intimate family interactions are simply not possible with a curtain pulled to separate two families.

Surveys of maternity care patients show that almost seventy percent of these women prefer a private room during their hospital stay. Maternity programs offering private rooms are demonstrating positive results from this nurturing environment. Family-centered maternity care options promote and facilitate family intimacy and interactions. A private room for the family allows it all to happen. Utilizing any of the desired options with the audience of a roommate and her family is stifling and inhibiting.

The private room also facilitates more quality, holistic medical interaction and less intervention. Nurses and physicians report that patients more readily share very personal medical or social problems in the privacy of their own room.

Patient Interaction

Women desire a private room during their maternity care stay, but they also want options for socialization with other patients. As much as women value privacy, they also want program options that provide social interaction with other patients and help to build relationships among patients with common interests and backgrounds. Facilities are responding to this need with different types of communal areas.

Family lounges, if available, need to be large enough to accommodate heavy utilization by visitors. Early labor lounges are popular with and useful for mothers in labor and immediate family. Patios with tables and chairs tend to be well utilized where weather and space permit. Nourishment centers where a coffee pot is always on and juice, fruit, and snacks are available can provide brief social contact among patients. Perhaps the most utilized communal area is a patient dining room. A continental or buffet breakfast can be served there to all mothers who wish to eat together instead of receiving a tray in their room. Buffet lunch or individual trays can also be served in the dining room. Mothers can bring their infants if they wish and share experiences—as new mothers like to do. These rooms are very popular, and long-term friendships have been formed from the socializing that occurs. Patient dining rooms can also be used for group classes at other times.

Follow-Up Care

It is worthwhile to provide home visits or telephone follow-up after discharge, which can improve care, identify problems in the home, and please families.

Families respond positively to follow-up care from the hospital where their childbirth experience occurred. Hospital staff have traditionally invited new parents to call the maternity unit if they had questions or problems following discharge, and public health agencies have provided postpartum home visits on referral. However, telephone follow-up initiated by hospital staff or hospital-based home care provided within five days after discharge has evolved primarily from an identified need to monitor the progress of early discharge maternity families.

It is effective to utilize nurses from the hospital maternity staff to provide home visits in the immediate postpartum period. The nurses first get to know the family and interact with the mother during the hospital stay in preparation for discharge. Communication among nurses who are working closely with the family during the birth experience is also easily accomplished. As a result, the continuity of care for both mother and infant between hospital and home is enhanced.

An added advantage to using maternity unit nurses for home care in the first five days after birth is their high level of skill. The nursing assessment and care capabilities required in this extended postpartum time frame are the same as those used continually during the inpatient hospital stay. Assessment skills in recognizing subtle signs in the neonate are the most critical for ensuring appropriate follow-up care when necessary. Home visits can also be provided by other hospital staff on the condition that they are well-trained and capable of answering questions and identifying problems or complications.

Home care and follow-up as described above are so popular with families that they are now viewed by hospitals as a positive marketing tool, as well as a valuable clinical monitor.

Single-Room Maternity Care

Parents value the elimination of the transfer of the mother in labor and her family from one room to another during the childbirth process. The equipment is moved from room to room instead.

The option of remaining in one private hospital room from admission to discharge has been one of the most popular changes for today's maternity care patient. The advantages are especially identified by the multiparous woman who has previously experienced a traditional maternity setting in which she was moved several times during the birth experience.

The decrease in transfer from room to room was initiated in the early days of birthing rooms. Low-risk families, who viewed the birthing room as an acceptable and safe alternative to home birth, also often wanted a shortened postpartum stay. They could labor, deliver, and recover in one room, then be discharged from this same room.

Innovative maternity programs now eliminate or minimize the multiple transfer system. Single-room maternity care provides an entire system of childbearing rooms in which the birth event from admission to discharge (excluding cesarean delivery) can occur in the family's private room. Programs utilizing LDR and LDRP rooms often require one move following delivery to a traditional postpartum room, depending on factors such as room availability and length of stay.

Mothers willingly state the positive factors associated with having their own family room. They desire elimination of even one move, if possible. Positive comments about the lack of transfer refer to feelings of greater relaxation due to the knowledge that the room "is their space" and that they can unpack their bags. Health care providers indicate that families using single-room maternity care systems have a shorter labor and postpartum stay and often require less analgesia or medication.

The availability of the multiple options described above and the flexibility that encourages and supports parents to exercise these options and fulfill their personal desires are what expectant parents of the 1980s want. None of the options will be desired by all people. At the same time, it must not be assumed that any of the options is so extreme that no one will choose it.[11]

We emphasize that including expectant parents in the decisions about their birth event does not mean or imply that the health care provider will surrender his or her professional role and responsibility. The challenge for health care providers is to look critically and objectively at medical care and management routines and policies. Providers must ask, What is the current, identified, scientific justification for continuing past practices? Are personal beliefs and values involved? If so, is it therefore inappropriate to influence a patient's decisions? Once the boundaries of safe practice are determined in any given situation, the physician, nurse, or other health care provider cannot be expected to cross the line into unsafe practice in order to fulfill patient requests.[12]

The health care provider must sit down with the patient and her partner, look them straight in the eye, and engage in effective communication. Good listening skills for nurses and physicians are critical. Patients complain frequently that they tried to express their feelings, wishes, and concerns, but no one on the staff seemed to hear them. Parents' questions must be carefully answered. Signs and symptoms of problems or scientific facts must be explained in detail, especially if undesired medical intervention may be necessary.

Sensitivity demonstrated by all health care staff members is essential for the family to feel positive about their birth event. Patients can have flawless clinical care, only to have it spoiled by one thoughtless, negative interaction with a staff member. This staff member may be a maternity service employee or an employee from another department, such as a housekeeper or billing clerk. The internal marketing approach to customer relations requires all patients and family members be treated as honored guests. It is important to convey an attitude of positive regard and respect for what families say and what they want, whether or not it corresponds with the physician's or nurses' opinion of what they should want.[13]

Expectant parents not only are shopping for options, but quality care at an affordable cost. Certainly, self-pay patients are extremely cost conscious. These families often utilize early discharge maternity packages for low-cost, yet safe, childbirth.

Cost is of less concern among women with insurance coverage. Some women state that since they are fully insured, cost is of no concern. However, more and more women are becoming cognizant of and influenced by cost issues, regardless of good insurance coverage.

The hospitals and physician groups that embody the philosophy of family-centered maternity care provide multiple options and flexibility to patients. They are sensitive and responsive to patients' needs and feelings, providing quality clinical care and helping to maintain lower costs in the marketplace.

NOTES

1. National Research Corporation, Omaha, NE, 1986.

2. Karl Albrecht and Ron Zemke, *Service America,* Dow Jones-Irwin, Homewood, IL, 1985.

3. Paul M. Taylor, "Parenting and Parent-Infant Attachment," *The Cybele Society Continuing Education Module.*

4. M. Klaus, J. Kennel, S. Roberson, and R. Sosa, "Effects of Social Support during Parturition on Maternal and Infant Morbidity," *British Medical Journal,* 293 (1986): 585–587.

5. J. Robert Wilson, "Obstetric Care, The Effects of Consumerism," *Postgraduate Medicine* 75 (1984): 15–26.

6. Diane Mason, "Options in Hospital Births," *American Baby,* March 1986, pp. 49–53.

7. Karl Albrecht and Ron Zemke, *Service America,* Dow Jones-Irwin, Homewood, IL, 1985.

8. M. Horn and J. Marin, "Creative Grandparenting. Bonding the Generations," *Journal of Obstetric, Gynecologic, and Neonatal Nursing* 14 (1985): 233–236.

9. M.L. Olson, "Fitting Grandparents into New Families," *Maternal/Child Nursing* 6 (1981): 419.

10. Susan McKay and Celeste R. Phillips, *Family-Centered Maternity Care,* Rockville, MD: Aspen Publishers, Inc., 1984, p. 38.

11. Judith Lumley, "Assessing Satisfaction with Childbirth," *Birth* 12 (Fall 1985): 141–144.

12. David A. Grimes, "How Can We Translate Good Science into Good Perinatal Care?" *Birth* 13 (1986): 83–90.

13. Karen Stolte, "Postpartum 'Missing Pieces': Sequela of a Passing Obstetrical Era?" *Birth* 13 (1986): 100–103.

Chapter 5

Single-Room Maternity Care

5

The onset of competition in the health care marketplace, coupled with pressures from third party reimbursers to decrease length of stay and overall cost, has forced hospitals to search for methods to lower operating costs and achieve a pre-eminent position in the community. One programmatic and physical plant change many hospitals are making is the conversion of traditional obstetric departments to single-room maternity care systems or other innovative changes in the way maternity care is provided.

The authors have worked with many hospitals to make such changes, and in fact, helped codevelop the single-room maternity care system several years ago.[1] Experience with single-room maternity care, in both large and small hospitals, has demonstrated that this system is capable of substantially reducing operating costs while increasing obstetrical volumes.[2]

Single-room maternity care is a total system that has proven to increase clinical response time, satisfy parents, and decrease costs. According to some experts in the obstetric field, single-room maternity care is the most advanced state-of-the-art care provided today. Single-room maternity care does not simply add LDR or LDRP rooms to a traditional obstetric department. Rather, it is a comprehensive system for providing individual patient care that utilizes private childbearing rooms for labor, delivery, recovery and postpartum care for the majority of deliveries, i.e., those of low-risk patients. Traditional delivery/operating rooms are utilized to provide care for the small number of high-risk deliveries, with recovery and postpartum care for these patients provided in a postpartum room located adjacent to the childbearing rooms.

Currently in the United States, over one hundred traditional obstetric departments have been renovated or rebuilt into single-room maternity care units. Many more such units are being developed throughout the country and are scheduled to open within the next 12 to 15 months. These units range in size from six childbearing rooms (in hospitals with small obstetrical volumes) to sixty childbearing rooms (in hospitals delivering several thousand babies each year).

Single-room maternity care units focus on family-oriented care, maintaining safety and clinical expertise while increasing family interaction through specialized programs and private childbearing rooms. The private childbearing room is a key feature of the single-room maternity care unit. Several years ago, maternity care providers recognized the importance to families of providing privacy during the birth process. Thus, in order to provide truly family-centered maternity care, a majority of the patient rooms in the single-room maternity care unit are private. A small number of semiprivate rooms are available for antepartum patients or other patients who do not desire a private room. In spite of the increased number of private rooms, gross square footage is generally less than that of a traditional obstetric department handling the same number of deliveries.

The childbearing rooms must be large enough to allow medical personnel ease of operation without compromising the standard of care. Private childbearing rooms require less space than LDR or LDRP rooms, but are larger than a traditional private patient room. The minimum square footage required for a private childbearing room is 180 square feet, excluding an attached bathroom. Optimal square footage is two hundred and twenty-five square feet, with a twenty-five square foot private bathroom adjoining the private childbearing room. Private bathrooms are important to include. Some hospitals use shared showers between two childbearing rooms, which seems to be acceptable to patients.

Although each childbearing room is larger than the standard private patient room, the unique functional relationships within the single-room maternity care unit make the overall square footage needed often less than that required using conventional obstetric planning and design. The single-room maternity care system modifies and combines functional relationships throughout the department. By bringing together all functions within the obstetric department, a design has been developed that can reduce the total gross square footage, while allowing an increase in total volume of patients receiving care. Thus, maximum and multifunction utilization of all rooms is achieved, even with significant increases in patient volume.

Included in single-room maternity care systems are the following support facilities:

- well-baby nursery (and intermediate nursery, if applicable)
- patient education/dining room
- family waiting room
- antepartum testing area
- delivery rooms
- nurses' lounge and lockers
- physicians' lounge and lockers
- on-call rooms
- staff conference room
- equipment storage/utility rooms
- staff offices

The demonstrated results of this design function have cut costs dramatically in both new building construction and renovation projects.[3] Furthermore, additional savings are generated through changes in staff and equipment requirements. The savings per year for FTEs in a single-room maternity care system average $100,000 per unit. All hospitals with this type of maternity care delivery system are showing an increase in the number of deliveries per year.[4]

WHY CHANGE: A "MODEL" HOSPITAL

Hospitals are motivated to implement the concepts and design of single-room maternity care for many reasons. The primary reason is that single-room maternity care provides a way to decrease costs and remain competitive in the marketplace. The following scenario describes some of the typical circumstances of a hospital choosing to implement this system.

The model is an urban hospital that had a substantial volume of obstetrical patients (four thousand deliveries per year) in the 1960s. There was an active young medical staff, primarily affiliated with this hospital, who were actively working to build their practices. As consumerism began to have a significant influence on practices and policies, this hospital added a birth room and admitted fathers to the delivery room. Some form of modified rooming-in was added to certain rooms on the postpartum unit. A few years later, policies were further changed to allow siblings to visit their mother in a room adjacent to the postpartum area. Everyone at the hospital thought they were providing truly family-centered maternity care. Families sought out this experience and nursing staff tolerated the "liberalization" of policies and new members on the "team."

Everything went along fairly well until the late 70s. Then a change occurred outside the hospital. That change was the introduction of a more sophisticated woman consumer. She waited longer to have her first child and became more discriminating in her choices. She began to shop for hospitals and doctors and was willing to switch care providers if she was unable to obtain the services and care she and her partner expected.

At the same time, inner city hospitals, including the model hospital, began to lose obstetrical volume as outlying suburban facilities grew. The physician staff, who once had affiliated only with one hospital, needed to split their practice and open suburban offices if they wished to attract the young, affluent market. Many of these physicians allowed their obstetric practice to decrease as they became more involved with gynecological and infertility care. Not only did these services provide greater financial return, but the physicians benefitted from fewer nighttime calls.

The model hospital did not keep pace with the changing needs of its patient population. Little, if any, physician recruitment was done. The medical staff was aging and fewer physicians continued to practice obstetrics. The physicians who did continue held onto traditional obstetrical practice and resisted patient demand for more progressive maternity care. The result was a marked decline in obstetric volume and a nonexistent image for the hospital in the community.

In the 80s, the hospital with its traditional maternity care unit now finds itself oversized, overstaffed, and underutilized by physicians and patients alike. Obstetrical volume is at fifteen hundred deliveries per year and dropping annually. The obstetric department has become a bigger financial drain than ever before, but because of the hospital's mission and desire to provide full service to patients, the department still functions. In desperation, not wanting to close the obstetrics department, the hospital seeks a solution to its problems. In order to survive, the hospital must decrease costs, increase volume, and build a positive community identity in the maternity care marketplace.

At first, the hospital experiments by adding a few LDR rooms. Administration believes this to be a less radical step in redesigning the facility and one that will turn things around. Later, they discover that LDR rooms do not decrease cost savings and the increase in patients is minimal. A competing hospital "goes all the way" and opens a renovated unit with a single-room maternity care system, forcing administration to rethink its position and completely redo the renovated unit simply to stay competitive. The model hospital will manage to keep its maternity care department viable, but because of resistance to change, the hospital must continue to play catch-up with its competitors.

Many hospitals initially or ultimately choose a single-room maternity care system because of the dramatic cost savings mentioned above. The bulk of the savings are generated through improved staffing ratios, as well as improved use of ancillary staff. In addition, costs for capital equipment (beyond the installation period) are decreased. Overall unit operating costs decrease because of improved functional relationships within the unit. Less movement of patients within the system requires fewer personnel, less equipment, and reduced space.

While decreasing costs may be the driving motivation for implementing a single-room maternity care system, increased volume soon becomes one of the results. Because of the high interest and demand for this type of service, hospitals implementing a single-room maternity care system usually experience dramatic increases in total obstetrical volume. For hospitals making timely decisions, a single-room maternity care system provides a new and vastly improved image in the community, allowing the hospital to regain or maintain the reputation as the leading facility providing maternity care.

WHAT DO WOMEN LIKE ABOUT SINGLE-ROOM MATERNITY CARE?

Prospective parents and families seek out the care offered in single-room maternity care systems because of the high degree of family involvement and flexibility of policies. Women state they choose these units because they desire the assurance of having a private room and not being moved during the birth process. The average American woman is moved an estimated five times during the labor, delivery, recovery, and postpartum process in conventional obstetric departments. Some obstetricians believe these multiple transfers disrupt the normal labor process and contribute to dysfunctional labors. Physicians also believe multiple transfers increase the need for more medications during labor, because of the resulting anxiety women experience from changes in environment and personnel.[5]

Because the single-room maternity care system is designed around a private childbearing room, each woman is able to begin and complete her entire labor, birth, recovery, and postpartum experience in one room. Should she need high-risk intervention (such as a complicated or cesarean delivery), a traditional delivery room is available as part of the single-room maternity care system. Not only are all of the childbirth functions completed in one room, but because the room is private she can labor in a position she finds most comfortable and include family and support persons as desired. Since most single-room maternity care systems have nursing staff trained to perform multiple tasks and functions, increased continuity of care and education are provided to the mother and infant.

One important attraction to families choosing single-room maternity care is that one family member or support person is given the opportunity to be present throughout the hospital stay. Provisions are made in the private childbearing rooms for the patient's husband or partner to spend the night. A slumber chair or sleeper couch is standard in single-room maternity care rooms. Policies are written and support services created to provide guest trays or complimentary meals one or two times each day. Very often, small kitchens are built on these units so that family members can bring food from home, which they can store in the refrigerator and heat in the microwave oven.

Because single-room maternity care units are designed with women in mind, they usually are decorated to appeal to women. Women often make their decisions about which hospital to use based in large part on the appearances of the maternity units. This is not to imply that safe, quality care is not desired, but for many women, this is a given. To the average consumer, all hospitals appear to provide good maternity care. Thus, the deciding factors often include the special amenities and attractive well-decorated rooms provided at one particular hospital.

The most successful units have created an environment that is more homelike and less institutional. This is accomplished through the use of color, artwork, lighting, and the addition of fabrics and wallcoverings. Creative administrators will solicit input from local women on what they like and desire. This can be accomplished through sophisticated market research or by creating an advisory board of fifteen to twenty women of childbearing age. Having this group meet with an interior designer and describe the kind of environment they prefer before making any changes can lead to a more successful program and create positive public relations as well.

PHYSICIAN REACTION TO SINGLE-ROOM MATERNITY CARE

One of the most complex aspects associated with implementation of a single-room maternity care system involves participation of the medical staff. Typically, the medical staff will be divided on the merits of the system. This division or difference in philosophy of care tends to produce three distinct reactions:

1. conservative, traditionbound, resistant to change
2. more progressive than conservative, but verbalize no strong feelings about either position
3. progressive, supportive enthusiasm about the change

The more conservative members of the staff often wish to avoid change and will take the stance that the system is unsafe. They will argue that it compromises the safety of both the mother and infant because there is no such thing as a "normal" delivery.

Many, but not all, of these physicians were trained years ago, when childbirth was treated as a surgical emergency. They have little experience with progressive care to help them through a major change in the way care is practiced. Many of these physicians are uncomfortable with the educated, assertive patient of the 80s. They wish to retain traditional care as a means of maintaining control. It is important to support these physicians and their patients. A single-room maternity care system provides for this through retention of the traditional delivery room.

Generally, in a single-room maternity care system, traditional delivery rooms are used for only complicated or cesarean deliveries. But these rooms are also available for and easily accessible to the patient or physician who prefers such a setting for a normal vaginal delivery. After childbirth, the mother, infant, and father return to their private family room for recovery and postpartum care.

One of the most effective ways to manage concern and resistance from physicians is to work individually with each member of the medical staff. The project manager or nurse coordinator should take the time to explain the system in detail, answer questions, and assure the physicians that single-room maternity care takes away nothing and will not compromise the care provided. If preferred, a private childbearing room can function as a labor room, with a woman being moved at the completion of her labor to a traditional delivery room, and then moved back for recovery and postpartum care. All physicians should be assured that if they choose to deliver a woman in the childbearing room, they can gown and create as sterile an environment as desired.

The most conservative physicians envision single-room maternity care as a kind of "alternative delivery system" that constitutes giving in to patient demands and unnecessary consumerism. It is not that. Rather, it is a system that provides the structure and environment for a range of options and experiences that are not only clinically safe, but satisfying to patients and their families.

The second type of reaction from the medical staff is one of disinterest or noncommitment about the concept and proposed changes. These physicians neither outwardly support single-room maternity care nor resist the concept. Usually they feel that they have little power in the department and are somewhat peripheral to the decision-making process.

Physicians in this group do not necessarily like or dislike the changes occurring in society and health care, but feel resigned to them. Although they may recognize the benefits of family-centered maternity care, they do not feel compelled to speak out favorably or champion such a cause. These physicians need the same attention and education provided to the more conservative physicians. Gentle assurance that their particular style of care can remain unchanged is important.

The third reaction from physicians is one of open support and enthusiasm for the change. These physicians see the innovative system as a way to market and attract more patients to the hospital and their practice. They understand that if patients are satisfied with their birth experience, positive feelings will be reflected back on them as the primary care provider. These physicians are usually the ones who want to be involved in the planning stages in order to make the unit as innovative as possible. They are often tireless committee members and frequently will work to educate and move their peers to a position of support. These physicians are recognized as being progressive and forward thinking. They very often have more patients than they can handle. The offering of yet another option to please patients is viewed as a personal challenge. The project manager should meet with each of them as well, to make certain they fully understand the changes to be implemented and to foster their continued support.

Regardless of the reaction of the medical staff, staff members managing the change process must be sensitive to and respectful of each physician's point of view. Constant reinforcement and factual information may or may not dispel some of the major objections.

Often a site visit to an operating unit in another hospital can be helpful to dispel fears and answer questions. If this is done, it is recommended that both supporters and opponents of the proposed changes be sent to visit the hospital.

If the change to single-room maternity care is an administrative decision made regardless of physician support, the decision needs to be conveyed as diplomatically as possible. Often administration makes the mistake of telling the medical staff their opinion counts, while in reality administration is already committed to the change and only trying to bring the physicians along. This strategy may work, but it almost always creates feelings among the medical staff of mistrust and resentment, which can linger and create greater problems than existed previously.

NURSING STAFF REACTION TO SINGLE-ROOM MATERNITY CARE

Implementation of a single-room maternity care system requires changes in the nursing staff. The nursing staff will react to single-room maternity care in much the same way as physicians do. Some nurses will support the change and others will resist it. Often, the mere idea of change is threatening. Nurses, like all human beings, resist change. They cling to old policies because they provide predictability and a sense of security. For many nurses, these policies also give a sense of power. There is a growing body of information that provides insight into the personalities of individuals that choose nursing as a career. Many of them have a low level of self-confidence and self-esteem. Such individuals tend to derive a sense of power from being able to maintain control over patients and their families.[6] While this is certainly not always the case, it is worth keeping in mind when dealing with individuals who constantly resist change.

Because of the publicity about reduced costs related to staffing changes in a single-room maternity care system, nursing staff fear they may lose their jobs if the system is implemented. The degree of threat and resistance can often be attributed to insecurities concerning job security. It is important for management to communicate planned staffing changes at the beginning of the project. If the number of jobs will decrease, this should be openly acknowledged and plans developed for accomplishing the staffing changes and relocating nurses to other units in the hospital. Both poor planning and the lack of honest communication can be extremely damaging to the successful implementation of any planned change.

Another factor that contributes to resistance among nursing staff involves the threat of learning new skills through cross-training. Many of the nurses involved in the change process may have worked several years in only one area of the obstetric department. They will react to a cross-training program by stating their interest in only being a nursery nurse or labor and delivery nurse. For most hospitals, however, the greatest flexibility and cost savings will be through implementation of a system involving cross-training for the majority of the nursing staff.

If the new staffing plan does require total cross-training of the staff, these plans must be communicated and explained as early as possible. It is not enough simply to present the planned changes. The nursing staff will need and deserve to know the rationale behind the proposed changes. During the cross-training process, expectations must be made clear. It is important to provide support and positive motivation through discussion and other means.

Some of the nursing staff will be openly enthusiastic and eager for the change. They will see it as a way to expand and increase their skills and abilities. These nurses often identify with the patients and support the experiences that today's expectant families are seeking. They also understand what the change can mean for the hospital relative to its competition. They understand, too, that they will become more valuable to the unit and the hospital by supporting change and reacting in a positive manner. These women are usually eager to learn and will actually place themselves in uncomfortable situations to experience a new challenge.

Special attention must be given to the attitudes and competency of the nursing staff. Nursing staff in these units need to have a flexible, caring attitude. They must demonstrate a willingness to adapt policies in such a way that family needs are met, while safety is maintained. The single-room maternity care staff, if well-trained and educated, are the best public relations force the hospital can have. They are frequently the reason patients and families leave the hospital satisfied and later choose to return—not only for maternity care but for other hospital needs as well.

Many staff members do not fully understand the need for change. Although every member of administration is fully aware of increased competition and the resulting need for personalized, service-oriented patient care, often there is a breakdown in communicating this information to the employees charged with the responsibility of providing such care. Time must be taken to sit down with staff nurses (and all other employees, especially those in contact with patients and visitors) to explain changes, answer questions, and provide support on a regular basis. Unfortunately, few hospital administrators and managers engage in this process, yet it is essential, regardless of the system used to provide maternity care.

In addition, hospital administrators and managers must recognize that as demands for decreased costs and increased productivity become stronger, rewards must be offered to maintain morale and staff satisfaction. Maternity care staff should be supported by providing workloads that promote individualized, family-oriented care. Also, by providing amenities for the staff, such as an attractive, comfortable lounge or compensation for additional training, the message will be conveyed to nursing staff that they are important as individuals and to the business of the hospital. And in today's highly litigious society, cheerful patient-oriented nursing staff can sometimes be the difference between an angry, threatening family and a disappointed, but understanding, family.

THE BOTTOM LINE

The implementation of a single-room maternity care unit involves much more than merely redecorating the physical plant. It requires both a structural and philosophical change in the way maternity care is provided. The changes will be both upsetting and exciting to the staff involved. It is imperative that the project manager be an individual with "big picture" vision, who has the ability to offer genuine and firm support to both the nursing and medical staff during this process. Because the process of implementing such change can be an almost overwhelming task, this individual will need solid support from his or her superiors. This support includes not only assistance and adequate resources to do the work, but also tolerance for less-than-perfect decisions, allowing growth and education through experience.

A single-room maternity care system can not only benefit the obstetrical department, but also improve the hospital's overall image, increasing patient trust and loyalty. It is important to thoroughly and carefully plan the process of implementation and involve as many of the key medical and nursing staff as possible. All people react more positively to change if they feel a sense of ownership for the project and clearly understand the goals to be achieved.

NOTES

1. L. Fenwick and R. Dearing, "'The Cybele Cluster': A Single-Room Maternity Care System for High- and Low-Risk Families," Monograph, The Cybele Society, 1981.

2. Michael Nathanson, "Single-Room Maternity Care Seen As Way to Attract Patients, Cut Costs," *Modern Healthcare*, March 29, 1985, pp. 72–73.

3. *Ibid.*

4. *Ibid.*

5. Charles E. Flowers, "Women's Healthcare: Provider Philosophy," paper presented at Women's Healthcare: A Profitable Product Line Conference, Chicago, IL, April 14–15, 1986.

6. Marie Manthey, "Cutbacks and Shrinkages: A Means To Eliminate the 'Victim Mentality'," *Nursing Management* 17, no. 4 (1986): 16–17.

Chapter 6
Case Studies

Skip the Maternity Derby.

Come to The Family Birth Place at St. Francis – you won't be jockeyed from room to room. The birth of your baby will be a moving experience – not an experience in moving.

One room: yours. At The Family Birth Place, every new mother has her own room. A single, private room with a home-like atmosphere – equipped with everything you need for a safe, comfortable labor, delivery and recovery.

Room to share. Your own room is big enough to include your family. A comfortable place where you can share this very special time and get acquainted with your new baby in complete privacy. And, after delivery, it's your baby's room, too, so you can be together in comfort.

Come talk to us about planning your baby's birth day. Phone for more information, or for a physician referral.

Call 445-CARE

THE FAMILY
BIRTH PLACE

St. Francis Regional Medical Center
Shakopee, Minnesota

Case Study 1

The Family Birth Place, St. Francis Regional Medical Center, Shakopee, Minnesota

Facility Description

St. Francis Regional Medical Center is a 126-bed general acute care hospital. It is located in Shakopee, Minnesota, which is a second-tier suburb approximately twenty-five miles from downtown Minneapolis. It is one of thirty-five hospitals providing obstetrical care in the five-county Minneapolis–St. Paul area. Five of these hospitals ring St. Francis, each approximately 15 miles from Shakopee; two are large suburban hospitals, two are community hospitals, and one is a new facility that opened in April 1984. The latter was the last construction approved by the Metropolitan Health Planning Agency and is located in one of the more rapidly growing communities of the five-county area.

St. Francis Regional Medical Center is directly involved in heavy competition for market share in the seriously overbedded twin cities of Minneapolis and St. Paul. The hospital serves almost all area HMOs, and is a member of a multihospital PPO. It also participates in a regionalized perinatal system affiliated with Abbott-Northwestern Hospital, a Level III facility.

Motivating Factors for Change

The primary motivation for change was the desire of the administrative staff and the board of directors for a strong maternity program with a competitive edge. Obstetrics had long been identified as important to the mission and purpose of the hospital. Considering the already highly competitive environment in which a new hospital was soon to be added with a service area overlapping that of St. Francis, the goals of the program were minimally to maintain volume and optimally to increase it.

Research Prior to the Program Change

No formal surveys were done specifically with respect to the maternity program. Since approximately 1977, changes in patient care approaches toward family-centered care had gradually evolved in spite of a very restrictive physical environment. Consumer responses to family-centered options were so positive that the administration and unit staff believed strongly that single-room maternity care would be very popular with area clients.

A six million dollar building and remodeling project for the entire hospital was already in progress at the time the maternity program change was approved. In the planning process for this general building project, demographic studies indicated that local statistics were consistent with national ones.

Planning Process

Minor remodeling of the traditional maternity unit had been planned, budgeted, and assigned a position in the phasing schedule of the entire hospital building and renovation project. An obstetric consultation was completed in late October 1982. Immediately following the consultation, an administrative decision to change to single-room maternity care was made with board of directors approval.

The responsibility for planning and implementing the program change was delegated to the vice president of patient services. Other key persons in the change process were the unit head nurse, the chairman of the obstetrics committee, and an interim coordinator who was responsible for managing the operational details of the change.

The first task following the decision to move from a traditional care approach to single-room maternity care was to immediately begin work with architects and interior designers to plan the recommended changes. These professionals, already involved in the overall hospital building project, were readily available for discussions. Fixed and movable equipment requirements were identified and ordered. Speed in decision making was crucial, since the phasing time frame originally established for the maternity department remodeling had to be met.

Nursing staff at the unit level were included in the planning process. A core group was identified which met first to brainstorm and develop a list of needed changes. The target date for remodeling completion and program implementation allowed only six months of preparation. Once the list of needs was identified, a flow chart was developed and completion timelines were assigned. The chart was then posted and unit staff were asked to volunteer to assist with tasks of their choice.

Cross-training of the nurses was planned and implemented. Some of the staff already were skilled in working all areas of the traditional unit. The goal was to have all nurses on the unit functioning at or above the level of identified minimum expectations within six months—by the scheduled implementation date.

The chairman of the obstetrics committee was involved as issues pertinent to the medical staff arose. The committee was kept apprised monthly of progress toward implementation and was utilized for medical care policy and procedure revisions and decisions regarding equipment selection.

Remodeling began in March 1983. The unit opened on August 1, 1983, as the first operational single-room maternity care unit in the United States.

Total Square Footage

- Original department size was 13,745 square feet.
- Existing space utilized before the program change was 7,095 square feet.
- After the program change, utilized space was 12,077 square feet.

The original department design of the 1960s included twenty-four postpartum beds, four labor rooms, two delivery rooms, two nurseries, and support space. As the number of deliveries declined in the early 1970s, the department was consolidated to occupy only the space originally designed for the labor and delivery function. This space continued to be utilized until the implementation of the new program in 1983. All labor and postpartum rooms were extremely small. Early planning of the 1982–83 building and remodeling project allocated the entire original space of 13,745 square feet for the remodeled maternity care department. The change to single-room maternity care allowed a space reduction of approximately 1,700 square feet.

Project Budget

Because St. Francis Regional Medical Center underwent a major building and remodeling program, exact structural costs for the maternity unit are difficult to determine. However, costs that can be identified are:

Structural

General remodeling costs for the program change	$10,000
Remodeling costs for the childbearing rooms ($4,000 per room for three rooms, including plumbing, casework and wall coverings)	$12,000
Total:	$22,000

Equipment

General movable equipment	$ 8,000
Homelike furnishings for nine childbearing rooms	$ 7,300
Birthing beds (three)	$18,000
Total:	$33,300

Grand Total:	$55,300

St. Francis Regional Medical Center decided to phase the total completion of the nine childbearing rooms due to cost.

- Three birthing beds were determined to be sufficient to serve patients in labor at peak census times. Following delivery, as soon as the mother is up, the birthing bed is removed and a regular patient bed is provided. The birthing bed is then cleaned and put into an empty childbearing room in readiness for an incoming labor patient.
- Remodeling was completed in three of the nine childbearing rooms. This consisted of wall coverings and the addition of casework including a work counter with sink.
- Homelike furnishings were purchased for all nine childbearing rooms to create the desired nonhospital feeling.

Of the total six million dollars for the hospital building and remodeling program, $40,000 was designated for general remodeling of the maternity unit. There was no other identified budget for the program change. Every effort was made to stay as close to the $40,000 budget as possible, even though the scope of the project had changed with the decision to implement a single-room maternity care system.

Physician Profile

St. Francis Regional Medical Center is a primary care–based hospital with an average physician age of forty-two years. Four obstetricians and thirty-one family practice specialists deliver babies. This mix has not changed with the new maternity program.

Nurse Training Program

The first step in the cross-training process involved the identification of minimum expectations for RNs and LPNs in the new program. These expectations were then communicated to the staff and discussed in a series of staff meetings.

Individual nursing skills were initially reviewed regarding level of ability to function in each of the three traditional areas: labor and delivery, nursery, and postpartum. The data from this review were utilized to develop a six-month training plan.

Short, concise inservice sessions were used to present basic content essential for each nurse providing direct patient care with the backup and support of a skilled, co-assigned nurse.

Mother-baby care as a system of nursing assignment was implemented very early in the cross-training process. All postpartum/nursery nurses were assigned to mother-baby couplets. Those who were reasonably well trained in the care of both mothers and infants worked closely with those who were not as strong. A cooperative spirit between unit staff members developed. Nurses volunteered assistance with implementation projects and provided many useful ideas for changing systems, forms, and policies or procedures based on experiences working through the cross-training process.

Concurrently, nurses who needed to learn labor and delivery skills were given a basic review course. They were then assigned, with supervision, to low-risk mothers in labor. Owing to the small volume of deliveries at St. Francis, not all work shifts have patients in labor needing care. Therefore, labor and delivery orientation and training is assessed according to the number of experiences each nurse has had, instead of days or weeks worked. Past experience and skill development in labor and delivery care are taken into consideration. Thus, the number of experiences needed to meet minimum expectations may be less for some than others.

Presently, nurses beginning employment require one week of orientation to mother-baby care and an average of fifteen labor and delivery experiences to meet minimum expectations.

Resisting Forces

There were no resisting forces. A few physicians were skeptical about the change and assumed a "wait and see" attitude about the effectiveness of the childbearing rooms. Once they began delivering in the rooms, the skepticism vanished. In the three years since the single-room program was implemented, physicians have requested use of the traditional delivery room for normal vaginal deliveries only four times.

Factors Influencing Success of the Program

Philosophically the nurses were already promoting and providing family-centered, client-driven maternity care. For five years they had become more and more skilled at

listening to patients' wishes and feelings and, when possible, facilitating those requests. The major limitations were
those of space and lack of privacy for families. With the
program change and remodeling, physical space and
patient privacy were provided to match the existing philosophical approach to care.

The fact that no one resisted the change was a major
contribution to the program's success. Everyone involved
with the hospital, including the board of directors, was
excited about the program.

It is also believed that the number and quality of the
family practitioners at St. Francis Regional Medical Center had a positive influence on the change. The single-room
maternity care concept facilitates the family-oriented care
they provide, and most were enthusiastic about the added
family involvement that was possible with the new unit.

Deliveries and Full-Time Equivalents (FTEs)

Deliveries

Fiscal Year (Ending September 30)	Number of Deliveries
1982	733
1983	676
1984	733
1985	749
1986	746

FTEs (Productive/Direct)

Fiscal Year (Ending September 30)	Number of FTEs
1982	20.7
1983	18.1
1984	14.7
1985	14.2
1986	14.7

Retrospective Decision Evaluation

Patient acceptance would have been even better if all nine childbearing rooms had been completed with the initial remodeling. Adding wall coverings to all rooms would have minimized the headaches of staff trying to accommodate incoming patients' wishes. It was not uncommon for expectant parents to ask if "one of the pretty rooms" could be reserved for them or for patients being admitted to request a "pretty" room.

Goal Achievement

Three years' experience has demonstrated that The Family Birth Place has created a strong maternity program with a competitive edge. The new competing hospital in the area that opened in 1984 is doing approximately 150 deliveries per month. Other hospitals surrounding St. Francis are reported to have declining obstetrical volumes. The number of deliveries in The Family Birth Place, however, has been maintained.

Competition and third party payor involvement in health care decisions have forced many physicians in the area to seek privileges at more than one hospital. Some physicians encourage patients to tour several of the hospitals where they practice and select the program most desired. A significant number of patients choose The Family Birth Place at St. Francis Regional Medical Center following a tour or visit to the unit.

Case Study 2

The Birthplace, St. Mary's Hospital and
Rehabilitation Center, Minneapolis, Minnesota

The Birthplace
at St. Mary's Hospital

Facility Description

St. Mary's Hospital, founded in 1887, is a 495-bed, short-term, general acute care hospital. The associated 251-bed rehabilitation center commenced operations in 1969 and is known for its services in adult and adolescent chemical dependency treatment (which it provides on a national scale), physical medicine and rehabilitation, and short-term skilled nursing care.

Located near downtown Minneapolis, St. Mary's Hospital and Rehabilitation Center has nine competing hospitals within approximately a five mile radius; five of these offer maternity care.

Motivating Factors for Change

St. Mary's Hospital and Rehabilitation Center wished not only to retain its market share in obstetrics, but to regain some of the market share that had been lost in recent years. Deliveries had declined from a high of 4,751 in 1964 to a low of 1,267 births in 1981.

There was also a desire to better utilize space and reduce costs by increasing productivity.

Research Prior to the Program Change

The maternity department at St. Mary's had two birthing rooms prior to the program change. Twenty-five percent of all deliveries occurred in these two rooms when discussion about program change began. This fact alone was thought to be a strong indicator that women in Minneapolis would like single-room maternity care.

Once the concept of single-room maternity care was identified, several research studies on consumer perceptions were done. This occurred before beginning to market The Birthplace. A total of over 500 persons were surveyed in the following studies:

- a telephone survey of Twin City residents
- physician focus groups
- a Catholic lay and religious leaders survey
- a "thought leaders" survey

The surveys indicated that women preferred the new single-room style of care for the following reasons:

- more like home/very personal way to have a baby
- the opportunity to be constantly with the newborn
- more convenient to stay in the same room
- more private and intimate
- more family participation
- more relaxed, making the birth experience more pleasant
- more natural
- the same way she had her last baby
- more modern/a desire to keep up with the times

Planning Process

The catalyst for change was a Cybele conference held in Minneapolis in the fall of 1982. An obstetric consultation was completed in late October 1982, recommending the implementation of a single room maternity care system

The principal persons responsible for the project were the director of maternal/child health nursing and the senior vice president and chief administrative officer. An ad hoc obstetric planning committee, chaired by an obstetrician, was formed. Its primary function was to review drawings and provide input and suggestions for change.

One year was devoted to planning. Unit design occupied a major part of this time, since the project required major renovation of the existing obstetrics department. An architectural firm was engaged to implement the design provided by the obstetrics consultant. Another consultant presented an LDR approach for consideration, but it was rejected. Due to the size of the project, a Certificate of Need was required. Money for the renovation was available in funded depreciation, making a bond issue unnecessary. However, approval for the financial outlay was required from the finance committee and the board of directors.

Construction for the new unit began in September 1983. The Birthplace officially opened in April 1984.

Physician Profile

Information prior to program implementation is not available. In 1985:

- A total of ten obstetricians delivered 46.1 percent of all deliveries. The average age of these ten physicians is 54.3 years.
- Approximately twenty-five family practitioners delivered 11.1 percent of the babies born.
- Certified nurse midwives were involved in 22.5 percent of the total births.

Nurse Training Program

The training program during the transition was and still is a preceptor program and is conducted on the unit. The length of time required to train each staff member depends on the qualifications and previous experience of the nurse being trained.

Resisting Forces

There was no resistance to the project at the administrative level. In fact, the positive manner in which the proposed change was received by the finance committee and the board of trustees was gratifying.

Some of the nursing staff and a small number of physicians were resistant to the single-room concept. Nurses verbalized concern and demonstrated insecurity about the proposed change in the delivery of care. A small number of physicians spoke out against the change.

Factors Influencing Success

The change to single-room maternity care succeeded because of a number of factors, including the following:

- a well-conducted marketing and advertising program
- enthusiastic nursing leadership
- a traditional delivery room available for patients and physicians who prefer it
- the first hospital in the area to offer this alternative
- supportive medical staff leadership

Deliveries and FTEs

Deliveries

Calendar Year	Number of Deliveries
1981	1,257
1982	1,285
1983	1,255
1984	1,369
1985	1,624

FTEs (Productive/Direct)

Calendar Year	Number of FTEs
1981	not available
1982	33.6
1983	32.2
1984	25.9
1985	27.5

Retrospective Decision Evaluation

The early recommendations by the obstetric consultant included a nursery of sufficient size to care for seventy-five percent of the infants, anticipating that twenty-five percent of the mothers would want 24-hour rooming-in. Clients of The Birthplace have not utilized rooming-in as projected, especially at night. If starting over, St. Mary's Hospital would size the nursery for one hundred percent capacity of expected postpartum census.

If provided the luxury of new space instead of dealing with the constraints of remodeled space, a nursing conference room and patient dining room would be added.

Goal Achievement

All of the desired outcomes that were identified before the program change are being demonstrated:

- The number of deliveries has increased by forty-one percent since 1981.
- The space the maternity unit occupies is 6,820 square feet less than that of the previous traditional unit.
- Nursing full-time equivalents have dropped significantly.
- Questionnaires utilized for patient and community feedback continue to be very positive and indicate the high public acceptance of the single-room program.

Case Study 3

The Birthplace, Mercy Hospital, Portland, Maine

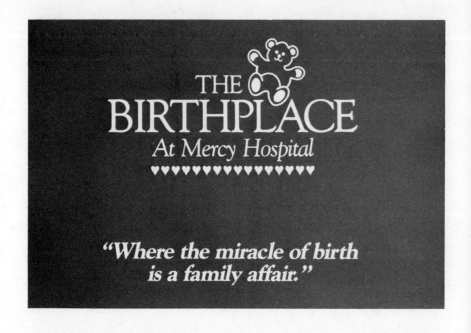

THE
BIRTHPLACE
At Mercy Hospital
♥♥♥♥♥♥♥♥♥♥♥♥♥♥♥

*"Where the miracle of birth
is a family affair."*

Facility Description

Mercy Hospital, sponsored by the Sisters of Mercy, is a 200-bed, private, nonprofit acute care community hospital. It provides inpatient and outpatient medical, surgical, pediatric, obstetric, and gynecologic services to 200,000 people in the greater Portland community. Mercy Hospital has competition for its market share from a major medical center and two other community hospitals.

Motivating Factors for Change

For many years the number of babies born at Mercy Hospital stayed at a low of 350 to 450 deliveries annually. The board of trustees and the administrative staff of the hospital had made several attempts to increase the obstetrical service volumes. All attempts to increase the number of deliveries at Mercy Hospital and/or attract new members to the medical staff met with failure. Because the hospital believed the obstetrical service was important to the overall mission of the hospital, alternatives to the traditional obstetric approach were pursued. The hospital, following an obstetrical consultation, pursued the single-room maternity care concept because:

- There was a need for a "Catholic alternative" to some current obstetrical practices.
- Comprehensive family care through all the stages of life is central to the mission of Mercy Hospital.
- Giving birth—because it is such a personal and family event—is particularly consonant with the objectives of Mercy Hospital.
- A sufficient number of deliveries are needed for nursing staff to maintain their skills.
- Delivering a baby at Mercy Hospital might create loyalty to the hospital for other family needs and future admissions.
- An increase in the number of paying private clients was needed to offset the expense of caring for a large clinic population.
- A mostly unmet need existed in the community for family-centered maternity care, i.e., maternity care that treats childbirth as a normal family event, rather than a health crisis for the mother.

Research Prior to the Program Change

No formal surveys were done to determine what the community response would be to a family-centered obstetrical unit. Mercy Hospital decided to change the program after many years of planning by the administrative staff and the board of trustees. As early as 1980, the Long Range Planning Committee of the hospital's board of trustees created a subcommittee on obstetrics. It was made up of board members, administrative staff, members of the medical staff, and members from the community. This subcommittee, after many meetings, recommended:

- encouraging all obstetricians and family practice physicians in the community to use Mercy Hospital for other than high-risk deliveries
- establishing a goal of 800 deliveries by 1983 and 1,000 deliveries by 1985
- implementing "family-centered maternity care" (this was not defined)
- providing obstetrical experience for family practice residents
- joint planning with other hospitals
- embarking on a public relations campaign
- providing education and upgrading the skills of obstetric nursing staff

The Long Range Planning Committee recognized that the above recommendations were not universally accepted even by members of the subcommittee (the medical community was lukewarm at best to the concept of family-centered maternity care). The Committee determined that they needed to emphasize the importance of obstetrics. They were able to do this because of a building program that was occurring at that time. A pre-eminent position for the program was created when plans were made to strategically place the new maternity care unit on the first floor of the hospital and to build the unit large enough to accommodate 800 to 1,000 deliveries. The Long Range Planning Committee also continued to meet with members of the obstetrical community.

In 1982, a second subcommittee was formed. This committee consisted of members of the administrative and the

medical staff. In 1983, the subcommittee made its recommendations:

1. to appeal to the consumers through a promotion of
   family-centered obstetrics with the emphasis on
   Mercy Hospital as a more private and personal alternative to the busy teaching hospital within the community
2. to appeal to family physicians and encourage
   greater use of service
3. to recruit additional obstetricians to Mercy Hospital

These recommendations led to the obstetrical consultation mentioned above. Following completion of the consultation, plans for implementing family-centered obstetrics in a
single-room maternity care system were begun.

Planning Process

The obstetrical consultation occurred on April 23 and
24, 1984. During this visit, a consultant met with the appropriate members of the medical community, the administrative staff, and the nursing staff. The hospital
determined that they needed new nursing leadership if in
fact single-room maternity care was to be implemented.
On April 23, a nursing division manager was appointed to
the obstetrics department. A nursing consultant was
brought in from June 20 to June 22. She met with members
of the nursing staff and began formulating plans for the
implementation of family-centered maternity care. At this
time, Mercy Hospital began to outline its change from a
traditional obstetrics program to a single-room maternity
care system approach. The nursing division manager of
obstetrics, with the support of her supervisor, the director
of nursing, and the director of clinical services, was given
almost complete control of the implementation process.
The change was handled as a special project; thus, report-

ing relationships were carefully outlined to allow for expedient decision making. Administration believed that if the change was managed by committee, the process would be too slow and the hospital would lose the competitive edge it had on neighboring hospitals.

Construction on the new unit began in April 1984. It was completed by November 1, 1984. There was no change in the total square footage of the unit, which remained at 12,352 square feet.

Project Budget

Because Mercy Hospital was in the middle of a building program, it is difficult to itemize the exact cost of the maternity program implementation. Most of the changes involved merely redesignating the functions of the various rooms. The estimated cost of the necessary changes in construction was $13,000. Equipment, furniture, and decorating costs totaled $124,244. The budget for the project was $142,000.

Physician Profile

In 1984, Mercy Hospital's obstetrical staff consisted of only four physicians: three male physicians and one female physician. Of these obstetricians, two were near retirement age and two were young physicians beginning their practice. Mercy also had family practice physicians who delivered a small number of babies each year. Since the opening of The Birthplace, Mercy has been successful in recruiting one additional obstetrician as well as attracting two other obstetricians who deliver at Mercy when they are not on call for the rest of their practice. At this time, there is a great deal of activity in the community with the potential realignment of obstetrical groups. Mercy hopes to attract new members to its medical staff within the next year. It is important to note that three members of the obstetrical staff originally resisted the implementation of single-room maternity care. The reaction of these three physicians to this type of care ranged from moderate disdain to active resistance. As the program was being planned, they stated they would be willing to try the concept in the interest of keeping obstetrics viable at Mercy Hospital. Since the unit opened, all four physicians utilize the childbearing rooms. Reflecting on the one and one-half years since the opening of the unit, the staff could recall the traditional delivery rooms being used only once for a normal vaginal delivery requested by the patient.

Nurse Training Program

All nurses beginning employment at The Birthplace go through an eight-week orientation program. The eight-week program is given to all new members of the nursing staff regardless of previous obstetrical experience. If a nurse has prior labor and delivery experience, the training includes a review of Mercy Hospital's protocols for labor and delivery, but with the major portion of training spent on infant and postpartum care. Basically the same training program is conducted for experienced nursery nurses, except that the program is altered to include more labor and delivery experience. The cost of orientation is equal to the weekly salary of the nurse, which on the average is about $9.50 per hour. The orientation is strictly clinical, with no classroom time included. This same eight-week orientation program was used for cross-training staff during the original implementation of single-room maternity care.

Resisting Forces

Other than the members of the obstetric medical staff, there was no resistance to the implementation of family-centered maternity care and single-room care. Support was received from the administrative staff, nursing leadership, board of trustees, and hospital employees in general.

Factors Influencing the Success of the Program

Much of Mercy Hospital's success can be attributed to the fact that a need for a more innovative approach to maternity care existed in the community.

The manner in which the program was implemented was also a factor influencing its success. Two change agents were designated to complete the entire process: the nursing division manager of the obstetrics department, who had primary responsibility, and her supervisor for this project, the director of clinical services. They were able to implement the program quickly and efficiently.

Deliveries and FTEs

Deliveries

Fiscal Year (Ending June 30)	Number of Deliveries
1984	385
1985	589
1986	672

FTEs (Productive/Direct)

Fiscal Year (Ending June 30)	Number of Deliveries
1984	20.5
1985	20.3
1986	20.3

Retrospective Decision Evaluation

The design called for a change room for fathers and an admitting-examination room to be located at the entrance to the unit. Neither of these rooms is utilized as intended. Fathers change when necessary in the private childbearing rooms. Examinations and admitting functions are both done in the private childbearing rooms when needed. If starting over, Mercy Hospital would combine these two rooms into one for an outpatient testing center.

The only other change would be to request additional funds for patient education and staff education materials.

Goal Achievement

One hundred eighty-two patient questionnaires completed approximately one year after implementation are overwhelmingly positive about The Birthplace at Mercy Hospital and the family-centered maternity care provided there.

Although other formal surveys have not been done, the staff at Mercy Hospital feel their goals have been met. The program has:

- provided the community with a unique maternity care program
- consistently met the hospital's mission of providing family-oriented maternity care
- increased the number of private clients
- created loyalty to Mercy Hospital in the community
- become a positive factor in attracting new medical staff
- increased the obstetrical volume by 74 percent from 1984 to 1986 while keeping staffing costs relatively constant

Case Study 4

The Family Birth Place, Jeannette District
Memorial Hospital, Jeannette, Pennsylvania

THE
FAMILY
BIRTH PLACE
Jeannette District
Memorial Hospital

Facility Description

Jeannette District Memorial Hospital is a 208-bed full-service community hospital located in Jeannette, Westmoreland County, Pennsylvania. The county is scattered with small towns and villages with a backdrop of rolling hills—snowcovered in winter, blooming in spring, lush green in summer, and ablaze with color in autumn. Jeannette District Memorial Hospital is one of five hospitals serving Westmoreland County and is the second largest employer in the city of Jeannette.

In addition to traditional acute care services, Jeannette District Memorial Hospital supports Pennsylvania's first single-room maternity care unit and Westmoreland County's only inpatient rehabilitation unit.

Motivating Factors for Change

Competition for obstetrical services within Westmoreland County is very high, with one hospital located only five blocks away and five other hospitals within a thirty minute drive. Recognizing this "duplication of services," the Health Systems Agency in 1976 recommended closing the OB Unit at both Jeannette District Memorial Hospital and another area facility. However, community concern and reaction to such action kept both units operational.

Although births at Jeannette District Memorial Hospital stabilized during the intervening years to an average of about one delivery per day, the operating loss of maintaining the department continued to increase, amounting to over $250,000 per year. Furthermore, when Jeannette District Memorial Hospital became a part of the newly formed Southwest Health System in July 1984, some system board members believed that maternity services should be consolidated at the sister hospital five miles away.

Jeannette District Memorial Hospital desired to continue maternity services under two conditions:

1. The service and care provided had to be safe and of high caliber.
2. The unit would not operate at a loss.

Research Prior to Program Changes

Given the motivating factors, as well as pressing space needs for the expansion of new and existing services, the board of trustees agreed to hire a professional consultant to conduct a marketing feasibility study regarding the maternity service. Accordingly, in December 1984, a consultant specializing in maternity services was selected to conduct a two-part study. Phase I addressed the maternity department's viability via analysis of departmental statistics, including occupancy rates, staffing patterns, area demographics, competitive factors, and the perceptions of community members, physicians, administrative staff, and trustees. Phase II included recommendations on strategies to resolve the problems and take advantage of opportunities uncovered during Phase I.

Problems and concerns identified with the service were:

1. High operating costs (creating a loss of more than $250,000 per annum)

    • staffing exceeded Monitrend peer group medians due to:

        —level of staffing to meet peak demands
        —lack of cross-training
        —station-fill staffing to comply with labor union contract

    • Excessive square footage as a direct result of decreased census

2. Low volume with no special features to attract patients
3. Because of low volume, there was concern about the quality of care (and resulting malpractice risk)
4. Lack of an adequate physician complement
5. Wavering in recent years of the board's commitment to continue the service, resulting in:

    • confusion in the community about the hospital's commitment to continue the service

    • a negative effect of confusion on community response to both the obstetrical service and the hospital as a whole

6. The hospital's role as part of a newly formed health system with a sister hospital also providing obstetric services
7. The possibility for implementing a rehabilitation program existed, but space was only available through either:

    • new construction

    • giving up the OB service and using its location in the hospital

8. Repeatedly expressed strong sentiment in the community to maintain the obstetric service
9. Closure of the obstetric service had come to symbolize the beginning of a movement toward the elimination of the hospital as a full service community hospital

Solutions were complex and multifaceted because of the many variables involved, including strong sentiment expressed by the community for an OB service, coupled with the need to develop a high-quality, cost-conscious program. The solutions included the following:

- Design and implement a single-room maternity care unit.
- Move the obstetric service to a smaller area and utilize an operating room in the OR suite for cesarean deliveries, multiple births, and traditional deliveries (thus increasing OR utilization).
- Free up existing obstetric space for a new rehabilitation unit, saving approximately $500,000 against new inpatient construction costs.
- Implement an extensive education and cross-training program to enhance and maintain the skill level of the nursing staff.
- Accelerate the physician recruitment program.
- Develop and carefully execute a marketing program to announce the new service and establish strong community support while expanding the hospital's service area.

Planning Process

Once the board of trustees of Jeannette District Memorial Hospital and the Southwest Health System approved the consultants' recommendations, the assistant administrator was named chairman of a task force charged with implementing the new program as quickly as possible. Task force members included the medical staff chief of OB/GYN, director of finance, director of nursing, OB nursing supervisor, obstetrics head nurse, coordinator of maternal and child education, associate director of system communications, coordinator of public relations, and director of materials management. Time became a critical factor because the space being vacated by the old maternity department was to be converted to a new rehabilitation unit, which had to admit its first patient by mid-July or risk losing one full year's reimbursement.

The associate director of system communications was given primary responsibility for working with the consultants to plan and implement the marketing plan, with only two months from approval to the opening date.

Nursing consultants were utilized to assist with the development and implementation of cross-training, establishment of new unit staffing methods, and single-room maternity care strategies. Since Jeannette District Memorial Hospital was the first hospital in Pennsylvania to implement the single-room maternity care system, a close working relationship with the State Department of Health to establish new regulations and guidelines was necessary.

The board of trustees decision was made on February 26, 1985. Remodeling began April 15, 1985, and the unit opened May 22, 1985.

Total Square Footage

- Before the program change was 15,273 square feet.
- After the program change was 4,537 square feet.

Project Budget

	Budget	Actual
Remodeling		Done on $185,950
		time-and-
Equipment/Furniture		material basis.

Physician Profile

In 1984, three obstetricians and no family practitioners were practicing obstetrics at Jeannette District Memorial Hospital. Two obstetricians were recruited in conjunction with the development of the new single-room maternity care unit. One obstetrician left the hospital for personal reasons, but another, from a competing hospital, has joined the medical staff. The current complement of active physicians consists of five obstetricians and four family practitioners.

Nurse Training Program

From the program decision to implementation of the single-room maternity care system, the maximum time available to prepare nursing staff for the perinatal nursing role was three months. As soon as the program decision was made, a cross-training nursing consultation was obtained and a full-time unit nursing position for education was designated.

The skill level of each staff member was assessed and the cross-training was completed specific to each individual's needs. Fortunately, many of the nurses were already able to function in at least two of the three areas of traditional maternity care. Only three staff members had no labor and delivery experience.

Various methods of teaching were utilized, including:

- Self-learning modules were utilized.
- Inservices and skills labs were provided on-site.
- Class content was provided at Jeannette District Memorial Hospital by the Western Pennsylvania Perinatal Education Council.
- Some staff nurses were sent to Western Pennsylvania Hospital in Pittsburgh (a Jeannette District Memorial Hospital referral facility) for nursery and/or labor and

delivery experience, that included didactic, observation, and hands-on nursing care. Time spent at Western Pennsylvania Hospital varied according to individual need; some as little as two days, some as much as two weeks.

Three nurses left the staff voluntarily during the change process. All remaining staff met minimum performance expectations at the time of single-room maternity care implementation.

Resisting Forces

There were essentially no resisting forces. To the contrary, the board of trustees, administrative staff, and medical staff were totally committed to and enthusiastic about the change. It must be remembered that in 1976 the HSA had recommended that Jeannette District Memorial Hospital close the maternity department. Everyone recognized the need to keep it open for the long-term viability of other patient services. Thus the change served as a symbol of survival.

Factors Influencing Success

- Enthusiastic leadership which was contagious to all concerned
- Community support, demonstrated by a record turnout of the public at the official unit open house
- First and only unit of its kind, to date, approved by the Pennsylvania State Department of Health
- Increased patient interest, demonstrated by over one thousand inquiries (by telephone and letter) in the first two months
- General increase in morale and motivation of the maternity care staff, as well as total hospital staff

- Decreased direct and indirect costs, which were passed on to patients in lower charges

Deliveries and FTEs

Deliveries

Fiscal Year (Ending June 30)	Number of Deliveries
1984	366
1985	315
1986	375
Projected 1987	400+

FTEs (Productive/Direct)

Fiscal Year (Ending June 30)	Number of FTEs
1984	22.25
1985	20.36
1986	14.6
Projected 1987	14.6

Retrospective Decision Evaluation

If the space were available, the childbearing rooms and the nurses' station would be made slightly larger. However, the constraints of existing square footage made this impossible in the current area.

Goal Achievement

The maternity program change has achieved the following positive results:

- The Family Birth Place came close to breaking even in the fiscal year 1986 (ending June 30), even with marketing expenses of $70,000. It is projected that the unit

will break even or begin to generate a surplus in fiscal
year 1987.

• Jeannette District Memorial Hospital was the only
hospital of five facilities in Westmoreland County that
experienced an increase in the number of births in the
fiscal year concluded June 30, 1986.

Case Study 5

Single-Room Maternity Care Unit, Wake Medical Center, Raleigh, North Carolina

Pregnancy & Fitness

Wake Medical Center
3000 New Bern Ave. • Raleigh, NC • 27610 • (919) 755-8000

Facility Description

Wake Medical Center is composed of one main facility located in Raleigh, North Carolina, and four satellite hospitals located in four rural areas of Wake County. The five facilities are licensed for a total of 625 beds. The hospital has a large cardiovascular program and one of the only neuro ICUs in the area. The hospital is in the process of applying for Level II trauma status, and has in the past two years received certificate of need approval for a rehabilitation program.

The obstetrics department delivered 3,327 babies in fiscal year 1985. Of this total, approximately thirty percent were generated from a clinic located at the hospital and run by the obstetrical teaching service in affiliation with the University of North Carolina at Chapel Hill. The clinic primarily serves indigent patients through a contractual agreement with Wake County.

Raleigh is the capital of North Carolina and the second largest city in the state. The population, including the county, is approximately 325,000. Besides state government, the area is known for its high tech industry located approximately fifteen miles from Raleigh in the Research

Triangle. There are three major universities within a thirty-mile radius, and numerous smaller colleges. The current unemployment rate is between three and five percent. There are two active HMOs: Kaiser and Health America. Recently the physicians in the area organized a large PPO, which promises to slow the growth of the HMOs.

Motivating Factors for Change

A large obstetrics/gynecology group that practices only at Wake Medical Center serves twenty-five percent of the total Raleigh market. This one group delivers thirty-six percent of all maternity care patients at Wake Medical Center. The five physicians in this group provide a very progressive approach to maternity care and employ three nurse midwives. Because of the size of their practice, they have a strong influence on the obstetric service at Wake Medical Center. The physicians very much wanted a more contemporary, consumer-oriented environment for their patients. For a time, they investigated the possibility of building a free-standing birthing center adjacent to their offices. The consequences of such action served as a catalyst motivating the administration of Wake Medical Center to evaluate and assess the maternity services.

Another motivating factor was the continued growth in the obstetric volume at Wake Medical Center. Hospital administration recognized the positive effects on other services. Maternity care was designated as one of the services the hospital wished to develop as a "center for excellence."

Research Prior to the Program Change

No market research was done prior to making decisions for programmatic change to single-room maternity care. However, market research and analysis for maternity care and women's health care was conducted in the summer of 1986. The information gathered will be used in part to develop target markets for advertising and promotional campaigns.

Planning Process

Evaluation and assessment of the maternity service began in September 1983. Four months later, the hospital retained a nationally known consultant to design the physical plant and patient care program. Key hospital and physician staff were sent to visit two single-room maternity care units at other hospitals.

Approximately eight months into the planning process, a director of women-infant services, with experience in single-room maternity care, was hired to serve as project manager for development and implementation. At about the same time, one of the members of the larger obstetrics groups became section chief of the obstetrics/gynecology department.

In September 1984, Certificate of Need development and architectural design were initiated. Certificate of Need approval was granted in May 1985, and the ensuing twelve months were required for design refinement, equipment selection, bid process, and contractor selection. A ground breaking ceremony in June 1986 marked the beginning of construction. Project completion is anticipated in April 1988.

Key personnel in the planning process included the hospital president, vice president of patient services, director of women-infant services, obstetrics/gynecology nursing unit managers, and the vice president of plant operations. The medical staff was represented by two staff neonatologists and the section chief of obstetrics/gynecology. Architects and the maternity care hospital consultant provided professional guidance and assistance in the planning process. A maternal-child health ad hoc committee was formed for input.

Total Square Footage

- Prior to the Change: 24,518 square feet.
- After the Change: 32,610 square feet, with the addition of an office wing and solarium.

Project Description

The maternity care unit is part of a total new construction project for women-infant services. Included in the project are two administrative office wings, a single-room maternity care unit, a 28-bed intensive and intermediate care nursery, and a 33-bed women's inpatient unit. The single-room maternity care unit is a 39-bed system, with 27 private childbearing rooms and 6 semiprivate rooms. The semiprivate rooms will be used for repeat cesarean delivery patients and antepartum high-risk patients who do not wish a private room.

Project Budget

The budget for the total women-infant services new construction as described above is 7.5 million dollars. Separate costs for the single-room maternity care unit are not available.

The final cost is undetermined since the project is still in process. In the beginning phase, the steel bid was under budget; thus, it is anticipated that overall costs could be under budget as well.

Physician Profile

Sixteen obstetricians, three midwives, and one family practitioner serve maternity care patients at Wake Medical Center. The teaching service affiliated with the University of North Carolina adds obstetric/gynecology residents and two faculty obstetricians.

The obstetricians comprise four group practices, three of which practice exclusively at Wake Medical Center.

Nurse Training Program

The training process is planned and being phased in over a period of two years, because of the complexity and size of the department and the April 1988 projected completion date.

Beginning in April 1985, all nurses hired to labor and delivery who do not have previous experience in labor and delivery initially complete a one- to three-month orientation to postpartum and newborn nursery care, followed by labor and delivery orientation.

In May 1985, a two-hour inservice program was presented, teaching labor and delivery RNs to care for infants at the mother's bedside for two hours postdelivery.

Mother-baby nursing was implemented on one postpartum unit in October 1985. All nursery and postpartum RNs and LPNs, approximately 48 full-time equivalents (FTEs), are provided one day of didactic teaching and an average of two to three weeks on this unit. Mother-baby training is designed with a buddy system approach. As more nurses complete the training process, mother-baby care will be expanded to additional postpartum areas.

In January 1986, teaching of the Virginia Neonatal Plan was begun for all RNs in labor and delivery, newborn nursery, intensive care nursery, and postpartum. Approximately eighty-five staff members, at a direct cost of $50 each, will complete this training by February 1987.

Core skills, which will be expected of all staff on the maternity care unit, have been identified and presented. Evaluation of each nurse's ability to demonstrate these skills will begin in March 1987.

Resisting Forces

There essentially has been no resistance to the planned changes. Due to the hospital's position in the community as a "county" facility, administration has some concern about adopting some of the amenities that could make the unit stand out in the community and the region as a premier maternity center. The nurses continue to be excited and enthusiastic about the project. The physicians have been positive and supportive of the project throughout the planning process. Women in the community who know about the changes are excited. Newspaper articles have generated enthusiastic telephone calls inquiring about the proposed maternity programs.

Factors Influencing Success

Because construction is in progress, success of the program cannot yet be measured. However, factors that have contributed to a positive change process include the following:

- supportive senior administration and board of trustees
- contemporary, liberal, and forward-thinking physicians committed to progressive, family-centered care
- a strong vice president of patient services
- an experienced director of women-infant services
- contemporary and flexible nursing staff in all areas

Deliveries and FTEs

Deliveries

Fiscal Year (Ending September 30)	Number of Deliveries
1985	3,327
1986	3,365

FTEs (Productive/Direct)

Fiscal Year (Ending September 30)	Number of FTEs
1986	84.5

Goal Achievement

Orientation to single-room maternity care for the medical and nursing staff will be completed by the time construction is finished. Currently, the changes that have been initiated have produced the following results:

- Volume has been maintained in the obstetrical department.
- Members of the OB/GYN medical staff have been retained and new members are being recruited.
- The service has been consolidated and interim physical plant and patient care program changes have been made.

Chapter 7

Interim or Transitional Phases

7

The process of directing major physical plant changes through either renovation or new construction can often take months to plan and even longer to complete. The time that elapses between the inception and the implementation of major change is often critical to maintaining or increasing patient volume. Thus, in order to keep the hospital visible in the public eye while the major change is being completed, interim programming will be necessary.

During major change, to update and improve maternity care services, it is wise to develop patient care programs that can be implemented quickly, are market-driven, and enhance the patient care services image. Some of these programs may be small and can be established without much planning or expense. Others are larger and will serve as a foundation to support the proposed changes. As with all program change, it is important that key members of nursing, medical staff, administration, marketing and public relations work together to plan and develop the programs. Some areas where program development can occur are:

- education
- special services
  - —celebration dinners
  - —home visits
  - —early discharge

- mother-baby nursing
- price packaging

EDUCATION

A strong prenatal education program is an invaluable resource to the hospital. Such programs will enhance services for patients choosing a hospital and serve as a way to attract patients who might not otherwise use the facility. If classes are developed that respond fully to the needs of the market, they will enhance the image of the facility and support physician practices in the community.

Because of the large number of obstetrical patients seen by many physicians, it is not always possible for physicians to provide the individual teaching and counseling that many women require and wish to have. Reputable classes sponsored by the hospital supportive of hospital/physician philosophies are one way for a hospital to reach many patients. In addition, expectant parents attending a class at one hospital, but planning to deliver at another, will often make a change in their choice of provider based on the total family-centered maternity care program "discovered" through the special classes and programs. The authors recommend offering such classes as part of a package for families delivering at the sponsoring hospital, and charging a small fee to all others. At no time is it recommended that classes be limited only to families planning to deliver at the sponsoring hospital. The classes should be viewed as a mechanism to sell and introduce the hospital and its services.

Because of the potential for patients to change providers during their pregnancy, it is important to have programs that are not only well planned and taught, but also well administered. The individuals responsible for describing and ultimately selling these classes to the public must be positive and energetic on the telephone and have the ability to convey a warm image to the caller. To the caller, this person is "the hospital." It is strongly recommended that the individual(s) be given formal training and instruction prior to beginning their job. They must understand the importance of the job and recognize the impact of their work to overall program success.

Many hospitals receive telephone inquiries about the maternity care service or classes that are answered by volunteers or staff nurses. Volunteers with the special expertise described above can greatly benefit the hospital. It is best not to transfer calls for information to a patient care unit. Even with special training, the nursing staff are frequently too busy to adequately respond to a caller's questions. Worse still, they will often tell the caller they are too busy, thinking she will understand. She does not. Many women have described the annoyed feelings this kind of response provokes. Further, they often conclude that if a nurse is too busy to answer a few simple questions, the hospital is understaffed. Their ultimate conclusion: The hospital is not a good choice for maternity care.

Prepregnancy Classes

A discussion of some of the most successful programs in the country follows.

A Baby, Maybe?

This is a class or course offered to couples contemplating pregnancy. It is based on the concepts presented in a book of the same title by Elizabeth Wheelen. The class explores the psychosocial and practical issues involved in the decision to have a child or remain childless. The class can be offered as a one-night seminar or as a series of shorter sessions scheduled over a four to six week period. Participants report the information is best disseminated through the series and in small groups of six to eight couples. The class is also more effective if led by a group facilitator team composed of one parent and one nonparent.

This class has the highest appeal among middle to upper income groups, who tend to be educated and to value planning and control as a way of life. One target group that responds well consists of professional working women who have delayed childbearing to further education or pursue career opportunities.

If the hospital relies on dissemination of information about the class solely through OB/GYN physicians, responses may be limited. Direct mail, newspaper or television advertisements, and short presentations to women's groups will be far more effective.

Pre-conception Health Promotion

"Today's Choices and Tomorrow's Babies" is a three hour seminar designed to educate participants on optimal physical health prior to conception. Many obstetricians believe that significant reductions in perinatal and maternal morbidity and mortality can be realized if a pre-conception health focus is adopted. The information women receive will enhance care provided by the physician before conception occurs, assuring identification of risk factors and optimal health during the conception period.[1]

The class focuses on three major areas: (1) routine pre-conception health assessment, (2) patient educational efforts to reduce identified risks, and (3) accessable referral services to promote a high level of wellness prior to conception for women with special needs.

Because of the heavy emphasis on identification and prevention of risk factors, the class should be developed in close cooperation with the attending medical staff. At the completion of the class, participants planning to conceive within twelve months are encouraged to see their physician for consultation and counseling.[2]

Hospital brochures describing the maternity care program, educational classes, and attending physicians (obstetricians, family practitioners, and pediatricians) can be provided to all women in the class.

This class should be provided free of charge or priced low. It should be offered at times compatible with the schedules of both working and nonworking women. Offering classes on Saturday mornings and Sunday afternoons should be explored as an option. In addition to offering valuable information to community residents, such classes provide an excellent vehicle for the hospital to make contact with prospective patients. Effective programs can influence decisions not only about which hospital to choose, but also about physician choice.

Early Pregnancy

The time period between confirmation of pregnancy and classes for labor and delivery has long been overlooked as an opportunity to provide education. During this time, women and their partners are beginning to undergo not only the physical changes of pregnancy, but many of the emotional ones as well. It is an optimal time for helping families to change unwanted lifestyle and health habits and begin planning for the impending birth. During early pregnancy, many women are highly motivated to learn as much as possible about pregnancy and childbirth. The classes described below can be priced and marketed as a package or presented "cafeteria" style, allowing women to pick the ones suitable to their needs. Regardless of how they are packaged, it is important that information about classes and registration be readily accessible. Certainly it is useful to keep brochures in the offices of the attending obstetrical staff. However, other good places for brochure distribution are:

- maternity clothing stores
- children's clothing stores with infant merchandise
- daycare centers and preschools
- pediatricians' and family physicians' offices
- community women's centers
- community and grocery store bulletin boards
- church bulletins or newsletters

Also take advantage of radio and television public service announcements for classes offered at no cost to the public. These classes are an important vehicle for making contact with pregnant women during a time when the decision about hospitals for maternity care is being made. A well-designed program will capitalize on this, as well as advertise the childbirth options offered by the hospital. The following classes support this goal.

Nutrition and Diet

An important class for an "early bird" series is one that places an emphasis on nutrition. Not only do nutrition and diet provide the foundation for good health during pregnancy, but these topics are often given little time for discussion in the physician's office. A hospital maternity care program can support its attending physicians by offering nutritional education and counseling to women in the community. Almost all hospitals have a registered dietician on their staff who can teach such a class. One of the more innovative approaches involves providing participants with a detailed computer analysis of their diet based on a three to five day intake journal.

Participants will generally be interested in the major components of good nutrition during pregnancy and lactation, including a review of the basic food groups. (However, care should be taken to prevent the class evolving into "Nutrition 101.") Some classes have met for one session at a local grocery store, going through the aisles and noting the best kinds of food, including how to prepare them using fresh ingredients. Grocery store managers are usually eager to cooperate because of the visibility provided for their store.

One of the most creative and informative books on the topic is by Dr. Judith Brown, who is a nutrition specialist and a member of the public health faculty, maternal child division, at the University of Minnesota. Her book, directed to consumers, is a practical guide to nutrition during both pregnancy and lactation. The ideas presented in this publication can easily be presented in a one- to three-hour class on the topic. Of special interest is her approach to controlling weight increase during pregnancy.

Pregnancy Fitness

Classes on exercise and fitness have become a popular addition to an early bird series. Some hospitals are developing their own classes while others are purchasing franchised programs such as "Pregnancy Fun and Fitness"[3] or the program developed by SomeBody, Inc.[4] Whatever the approach, these classes should closely follow the guidelines for pregnancy exercise established by the American College of Obstetricians and Gynecologists. In addition, hospitals should check with legal counsel to ensure that liability waivers for participants are in order.

Women who attend these classes are frequently incorporating the class into an already busy schedule. For maximum success of the program, classes should be offered in several convenient locations in the community. This may require the sponsoring hospital to contract for space in a health club, YWCA, or community meeting place. Times of classes should be convenient to women working both in and out of the home. Parking should be safe, convenient, and free of charge.

Because women often begin these classes early in pregnancy, it is important to take great care in choosing instructors. These instructors become "ambassadors" for the hospital and often have a direct influence on the woman's participation in other health care programs and her choice of hospital for maternity care. Instructors should be of appropriate body weight, nicely groomed, and dressed in a manner suitable for exercise activities.

Many HMOs and private businesses offer paid education programs for their enrollees and employees. Prior to instituting a fitness program, an instructor or maternity care coordinator should meet with company representatives to determine if the program will meet guidelines for reimbursement. If so, this can be a strength in advertising the program and securing a participant base.

Infant Feeding and Preparation for Breastfeeding

Usually during the midmonths of pregnancy, women decide how they will feed their babies. Even with all the literature available about the topic, there is still much misinformation about breastfeeding. As part of the early pregnancy series, a two session class can be offered on this topic.

The first session focuses on the pros and cons of both bottle and breastfeeding. Mothers experienced with both methods can talk about their choice and the benefits and problems they encountered. Information on the role of nutrition in the development of the infant and toddler can also be provided during this session.

The second session is for women who have decided to breastfeed their infant. Information presented in this class will support their decision, including practical facts about breast preparation, purchase of a nursing bra, and how to freeze and store breast milk. Discussions should also focus on the problems and solutions for working mothers who choose to breastfeed.

There are many publications available to serve as resource materials for the development of this class. Participants can also be introduced to local and regional resources such as the LaLeche

League. If the hospital is fortunate enough to have a lactation counselor on the staff, this is a perfect opportunity to advertise this service as a special service for maternity care patients. Indeed, this counselor may be the ideal person to teach the class.

Sibling Education

Classes preparing other chidren for the addition of a baby are among the most popular classes offered by maternity care programs. Two approaches to this class are used. One focuses on the process of becoming a big brother or sister, and the other focuses on preparing a child whose parents wish him or her to be present at the birth.

Sibling education about the experience of having a new baby in the family is the most common and popular of the two classes. Generally, these classes emphasize such things as what the baby can do, the sounds it makes, what it looks like, and what happens to a family when a new baby comes to live with it. Feelings and experiences regarding sibling jealousy and reduced attention from parents are talked about with the children. A really creative instructor will also educate the parents about the feelings and needs of older children. Real life situations are presented and children old enough to verbalize are asked questions requiring them to explore reactions to these situations. Many classes include a "hands-on" experience of diapering a doll and touring the postpartum unit. Special coloring books, stickers, or T-shirts can be provided, with juice and cookies at the conclusion of the program. Some programs have incorporated a film, such as *Nicolas and the Baby*[5] or the muppet film *I'm a Little Jealous of That Baby*.[6]

Parents are usually asked to stay with their children during the class and are encouraged to bring cameras and take pictures for the baby's book. Many programs provide parents with reading lists of books about children and the effects of becoming a sibling.

As with all the classes, the personality of the instructor is vital to the success of the program. One very successful program is taught by a maternity care staff nurse who was one of six children herself. Many of the children coming to visit their mothers after delivery were as eager to see the instructor again as they were to see the new baby. Instructors are key staff to build community goodwill and assist in strengthening the public image of the hospital.

Preparing children to be present for the birth of a baby is a very individual activity. Most hospitals with a policy for sibling-attended birth usually prepare and teach each family individually. Two methods are commonly used to accomplish this task. The first method teaches the parents the core information the child will need to know about childbirth. They are provided with printed materials and assisted with explanations that will best help the child relate to the experience. Usually families choosing this option are very open with their children. They appreciate the opportunity for support and assistance, yet wish to prepare the child themselves.

The other method utilizes an individual "family conference" with a health care professional. The "teacher" covers basic information with the child about what to expect, telling the child, for example, "Your mother may make some funny sounds you may have never heard before" or "The baby will be blue when it comes out" or "The blood you will see is 'good' blood and a normal part of having a baby."

It is important to make certain with either method that the information is factual in regard to hospital practices and that it is personalized for the particular needs of the child and family involved. Families should be encouraged to discuss this option in detail with the physician who will be delivering their baby. If the mother is receiving care from a large group practice, make sure all members of the group are in agreement on all plans for the birth.

Prevention of Preterm Labor

There is a growing body of information on the causes and prevention of preterm labor. Hospitals are beginning to offer evening seminars to acquaint women and their partners with the signs and symptoms of preterm labor and the lifestyle changes that contribute to a lower incidence of prematurity. Such classes are often taught by a physician and nurse team and can be presented effectively to a large group. They can be held in a large meeting place in the hospital, a church, or hotel.

In developing a class on preterm labor, it is critical to have major physician groups in the community endorse the concept. Some physicians are not yet completely comfortable with the information and worry that it may increase anxiety in their patients.[7]

Late Pregnancy

Preparation for Birth Classes

This is the "classic" of all classes and still one of the most widely attended. Two of the most popular methods for teaching the class are Lamaze and Bradley. If the hospital does not currently offer these classes in their education program, a community assessment of resources should be done before adding them. In many communities, organizations like the Childbirth Education Association (CEA) and the American Society of Psychoprophylaxis (ASPO) may already be teaching the classes and have a large community following. Nothing will alienate these groups more than for a hospital to start its own classes in competition with the local organizations. Care should be taken to ascertain the strength of these groups. Determining if they are meeting community demand and how physicians and nurse midwives feel about the quality and reputation of the instructors will provide useful information when developing hospital programs.

If there is a strong community-based group, we recommend that the hospital negotiate with them, offering free space at the hospital as well as support with marketing and advertising. Childbirth educators have a strong influence on the lives of pregnant patients. They should be given time and attention by hospital staff and physicians because of their power to influence referrals. Many bridges can be built by cultivating these important relationships.

If these programs are not offered in the community, they should be developed as the foundation for all maternity care education. There is still some question as to the actual value of these classes in the overall outcome of the patients' delivery experiences. However, women across the country have been socialized to believe they cannot have babies without them. It should be noted that some consumer groups believe a hospital cannot provide maternity care education classes in an unbiased way and will therefore devalue hospital-based classes.

When planning these classes, it is essential to develop them around the needs of pregnant women and their partners at this time in the pregnancy. Make the groups as small and intimate as possible while balancing costs for providing the classes. All classes should include a tour of the facility. This is a perfect opportunity to promote special options and opportunities at the hospital. If the classes are open to anyone in the community regardless of where they plan to deliver, there is an opportunity to attract patients from other hospitals and influence their choice of birth sites.

Hospital Tours

Hospital staff sometimes overlook this excellent opportunity to increase awareness of their services and facility. Following are suggestions to help make the maternity tour more successful:

1. First and most important, the tour should be organized using one central telephone number for potential patients to call for tour information and registration. As mentioned previously, the person answering the telephone must have special training to answer questions in a pleasant, positive, and informed manner. More specifically, this person should be taught how to "sell over the telephone." She should also be trained to promote other classes in the maternity department.
2. The tour should be free. If the hospital charges for parking, arrangements need to be made to have the parking charge waived. The method for doing so needs to be simple and easily accomplished. Everyone in the organization must be informed of the decision to waive the parking charge and the system for handling parking for those on a tour.
3. The tour groups should be small. Having groups of eight to ten couples allows everyone the opportunity to ask questions and get them answered. Smaller groups also create a warmer, more personalized atmosphere. Having smaller groups may necessitate several tours per month. It is recommended to vary the times and days of the week to accommodate as many families

as possible. High interest and response to Saturday morning and late Sunday afternoon tours occurs in some areas.

4. Carefully choose and train each tour guide. Select individuals who will represent the hospital and maternity unit in a polished, positive manner. Tour staff should enjoy interacting with people and be well informed about family-centered maternity care. It is essential to hold an orientation session to train tour guides. Topics that should be included in the sessions are:

- appropriate dress and grooming for leading a tour
- factual information about the maternity care unit policies and procedures
- information and handouts about other programs offered
- up-to-date information on costs for both vaginal and cesarean births
- method of leading the tour—what to show and what services to emphasize
- instructions for setting up and operating a movie projector
- information on the important services or features offered by the competition and ideas for responding to questions about these services

5. After the tour is completed, participants can come together in an attractive room for more questions, light, nutritious refreshments, and a contemporary childbirth or parenting film. A packet of information about the hospital and maternity care unit can be given to each couple to take home. The packet should include a preregistration form and postage paid envelope. In addition, information on other community resources, such as car seat rental, breastfeeding groups, and educational resources not available at the hospital can be included.

6. Have the participants evaluate the tour by completing a written questionnaire. Ask participants to respond to a few key questions that will provide useful information for keeping the tour relevant and successful. The questionnaire should include space for name, address, and telephone number. The names

and addresses should be compiled alphabetically or by zip code for future marketing efforts.

7. Devise an incentive to reward tour guides. Some hospitals have found it effective to provide time-back. Each tour guide is given one day off with pay for every three tour groups conducted. This has made the process of recruiting guides much easier, and those involved are more enthusiastic about the job and the hospital. If time-back is not an acceptable option, then provide compensation in some form, for example, extra pay or a gift certificate for two at a good local restaurant after three to five tours are given.

8. Promote the tour in the offices of physicians and nurse mid-wives, in women's centers, childbirth education classes, pre-school facilities, and pediatricians' and family physicians' offices.

Maternity tours provide information about the services and options available at a hospital while positively portraying the philosophy of the hospital to the community.

Postpartum Classes

When developing postpartum classes, do not forget that the time following a birth is a busy time in the lives of new and expanding families. The motivation to attend such classes may initially be high, but will decrease as family and work routines create the need to establish realistic schedules. The young couple who attended every class prenatally may be overwhelmed after taking the baby home and have difficulty attending postpartum classes. Because of this, classes that are developed for this time period must have high appeal and there must be strong community interest and demand.

Additional Classes

Following are descriptions of additional classes that the hospital may wish to offer. We recommend some market research to gauge the degree of interest before developing these programs. Pediatricians and family physicians are an excellent resource for market information about the potential for these programs. Generally, the classes are very well received by communities.

MELD for New Parents

MELD stands for Minnesota Early Learning Design. It is a program targeted to first-time parents. Groups are composed of ten to twelve couples or single parents. The groups usually begin meeting approximately thirty-two to thirty-six weeks of pregnancy. The meetings focus on helping new parents find a comfortable way to respond and parent their children. MELD believes there is no right way to parent. The philosophy maintains that given the proper information and support, each parent will learn the skills and choices appropriate for their family. Four modules are taught. Groups meet every other week for twelve sessions per module. The program is designed to foster development of support groups formed out of the class group.

Because of the focus on education and preparatory planning, the MELD program tends to attract a more upscale, affluent consumer. However, the program also offers a program for teens, called MELD for Young Moms (MYM). For best results, it is recommended that the two groups be taught independently of each other.

Creative Play Classes

These classes are designed to teach parents effective ways to play with a new and maturing infant. Attention is given to creating a stimulating environment for infant-child learning. These classes are not intended to create "super babies," but to provide parents the skills to recognize normal developmental milestones and maximize the individual abilities of each infant as he or she grows.

Father and Baby Classes

Classes are intended to provide education and support to fathers experiencing the changes brought about by a new baby. Information is provided about infant care, growth, and development, and role changes with other children and parents. The Bank Street College's

Fatherhood Project in New York City has done excellent work in this area and is a useful resource in developing such a class.

Support/Grief Programs

Support groups helping parents respond to the grief associated with a premature, malformed, or neonatal death are very helpful classes. These groups are usually led by a social worker or psychologist with special training in this area. Groups are typically ongoing and couples or individuals attend based on need. The classes are provided as a service by the hospital, usually free of charge. They are especially beneficial if the hospital has a Level III high-risk maternity care program.

Hospital-based classes offer a service not only to its patients but to the community at large, for the classes will attract families from outside the hospital as well.

CELEBRATION DINNERS

Celebration or champagne dinners are one of the most popular and appreciated services for maternity families. They are relatively inexpensive to provide and create much goodwill among families. Some hospitals, like St. Joseph's Hospital in St. Paul, Minnesota, have created a special dining facility for parents. The hospital's special dining room was created just for the celebration dinners. It is complete with soft lighting, piped-in music, candles, china, silver, and special linen. The dinners are served to parents on the evening preceding discharge.

Other hospitals use a special cart much like those used for room service in an expensive hotel. The cart is decorated with linens, china, silver, and fresh flowers before being rolled into a patient's private room. It is nice to be able to offer wine or champagne with this dinner, but be sure to check local liquor licensing laws before doing so.

For families choosing an early discharge option, who do not stay in the hospital long enough for the dinner, some hospitals prepare a basket with wine, cheese, fruit, and a small bouquet or potted plant. Other hospitals put edibles in a medium-sized paper shopping bag color coordinated with the maternity care unit and with the unit's logo imprinted on the side. Both methods allow families to celebrate on their first night at home and create a positive impression of the hospital.

Another option is for the hospital to contract with a local restaurant for a special dinner. Couples can be given a specially designed gift certificate embossed with the hospital maternity care logo and the restaurant name. They can then celebrate at a time convenient to them. The restaurant staff need to understand the reason for the dinner and agree to provide the couple special treatment, compliments of the hospital's maternity care unit.

A celebration dinner is certainly not a major component of family-centered maternity care. However, as competition among hospitals continues to mount, such services and amenities create a distinction, making one facility stand out over others.

MOTHER-BABY NURSING

Family involvement and family-oriented mother-baby nursing throughout the maternity care unit is a key feature to market strongly to women. The advantages of this system in providing continuity of care and flexibility of policies and staffing patterns are many. Today's enlightened maternity consumer is searching for a hospital experience that offers unlimited contact with her newborn, providing the option to have the baby in the nursery as much or as little as she desires. A maternity care program that offers mother-baby nursing generally has progressive policies and a staff who understand the importance of meeting individual family requests and needs.

This style of care provides more interaction among the staff and patients. Since care is provided in the mother's room to both mother and infant as a family unit, the family benefits from the added teaching and dialogue that occurs. Nursing that otherwise is devoted to the baby in the nursery now includes the mother as a participant. Also, by caring for the family as a unit, the nursing staff become more involved and can better observe and understand the dynamics of each family. As a result, a higher quality of professional interaction and preparation for discharge is achieved.

Mother-baby care and the policies established can be structured to meet the needs of most patients. When developing policies, efforts should be made to limit the number developed. Policies should respond more to the standards of care provided rather than dictating requirements for families.

Mother-baby nursing requires all nursing staff be trained to provide care for both the mother and infant. Assessment of clinical skills, with training programs designed to eliminate deficiencies, must be implemented. In addition, some nurses will adapt to mother-baby nursing better than others. Nursing staff need to be flexible and willing to work with families to meet family needs rather than staff needs.

Mother-baby nursing can be provided on a traditional postpartum unit or as a beginning step in patient care program change following implementation of an innovative maternity care system. If mother-baby nursing is implemented with a philosophy that puts families first, there is no end to the positive public relations that can be generated, not only for the maternity department but for the hospital as well.

An example of this style of care exists on the family care unit at Fairview Hospital in Minneapolis, Minnesota. In addition to mother-baby care, the unit operates with a self-care philosophy. All sixteen rooms have double beds and more resemble hotel rooms than hospital rooms. There are no routines on the unit. The day is structured around the needs of each family. The only request made of each family is that they participate with the care of their infant, as no nursery exists on this floor. Although this may be viewed as an extreme of mother-baby couplet care, the unit maintains a full census, while the traditional postpartum unit is often empty. Charges on this unit are less than charges on the postpartum unit.

PRICE PACKAGING

As a way to increase the number of patients, many hospitals across the country are developing a price packaging strategy. Services are offered as a package with a preset package price. A typical package for maternity care might consist of:

- twelve hours of normal labor and delivery
- a fetal monitor
- intravenous fluids if needed
- a twenty-four-hour uncomplicated postpartum stay
- a celebration dinner
- a follow-up telephone call by a nurse on the day of discharge
- a home visit by a nurse on the third day postdischarge

Some hospitals include preparation for birth classes if they are offered by the hospital. Packages are most commonly designed on the basis of time following delivery, for:

- twenty-four hours
- thirty-six hours
- forty-eight hours

These packages can be discounted anywhere from ten to twenty percent lower than each service priced separately. This strategy is based on the premise that by increasing volume, any charges lost by discounting will be offset through the increased volume. Some hospitals have designed the package with only the labor and delivery charge generating revenue. The additional time on postpartum is, in some ways, viewed as a loss.

There are varying estimates as to the numbers of patients who will be attracted by price packaging. Hospitals that are located in communities of high unemployment or large student populations have found short-stay–reduced fee packages very popular. There is also a budding trend among families who have HMO coverage to leave the HMO for special or unique obstetric care, pay the expenses out of pocket, and return to the HMO hospital for pediatric or other care. If this trend continues, price packaging will be attractive to an even larger number of patients.

Developing price packaging strategies can help the hospital in other ways as well. It will provide the hospital a negotiating position to bid on HMO or third party payor contracts. It will also present to the community an image of more responsive and progressive care, even though many patients will choose a short-stay option.

HOME VISITS

In the future, hospitals that survive and succeed will be those that developed a service orientation to patient care. The more this philosophy can be cultivated, the stronger the hospital's position will be. Incorporating home visits to mothers leaving the maternity care unit is another way to please patients and improve care.

Nurses on the unit can be trained for and assigned to home visits. Often these visits can be coordinated with their drive to and from work. Arrangements are made for the visit prior to discharge. Each visit takes approximately one hour to complete, including the associated documentation. During the visit, the baby can be checked and questions from the mother and family members answered. (For patients living long distances from the hospital, a telephone call involving similar questions and information can be substituted for a visit.) Upon returning to the hospital, the nurse making a home visit can call the pediatrician and obstetrician, providing useful information to the medical staff.

By having the nurse come to the home, the patient is spared the task of bundling up the new baby to go to the doctor's office. This service can be used to recruit other physicians by providing it to all patients free of charge with delivery at the sponsoring hospital. Physicians seem to appreciate any service that reduces the time they spend in their office or on the telephone supporting new parents through the normal crises of the first days at home. In addition, the patients view the extra interest and attention from the hospital as a very special service.

EARLY DISCHARGE PROGRAMS

As the cost of health care increases, the price for maternity care will be the deciding factor for some families in choosing a hospital. While early discharge does not have widespread support among physicians, many factors influence patients to request this option, when both mother and baby are normal.

The American Academy of Pediatrics has published reasonable guidelines for physicians and hospitals to follow when establishing early discharge programs.[8] Early discharge is not for all patients; however, it is widely accepted among certain patient populations. The following characteristics describe patients most likely to choose an early discharge program:

- patients without insurance
- students
- unemployed parents
- private paying patients who wish to avoid the control of a hospital environment
- patients with other children at home, especially if the children are very young
- patients preferring a home birth
- patients who are uneasy or uncomfortable in a hospital setting

One of the important aspects of an early discharge program is the provision of follow-up care by nursing staff. As with the home visit program, the service of sending a nurse into the home is viewed by the patient as an added benefit. However, a nurse providing follow-up visits to the early discharge patient must have additional training in order to know how to obtain comprehensive histories and to do full assessments, as well as laboratory work in the event the baby is jaundiced. In a program such as this, it is important that continuity of care and communication be maintained between the hospital, the patient, and the primary care provider.[9] Services must be offered seven days a week and on holidays. For this reason, outside agencies and public health departments are not suitable for the initial home visit. Later, these agencies may be utilized and referrals made for follow-up or long-term care. In developing and planning the early discharge program, it is essential to involve staff members from medicine, nursing, and administration. It is also useful to involve previous patients in this process. They provide valuable insights into aspects of the program that health care providers may neglect or view as unnecessary.

CONCLUSION

Interim and transitional programs are meant to increase services and continue image development in the community while the hospital undergoes change. If a major physical plant change in the maternity department is being planned, these programs can work to minimize patient frustration and improve the hospital's image. All of the programs can be added as companion features to a maternity unit working to be more responsive to the childbearing families in its community.

NOTES

1. Sally Squires, "Getting Ready To Have a Baby," *Washington Post,* February 5, 1986.

2. "Week by Week, A Program to Prevent Pre-Term Birth," *Denver Post,* May 14, 1986. "Week by Week" is run by the Rose Women's Center, 4567 East Ninth Avenue, Denver, CO.

3. Pregnancy Fun and Fitness Childbirth Education Association, 5675 Eastex Freeway, Suite 104, Beaumont, TX 77706.

4. SBI Maternity Fitness Program, 2 Bala Plaza, Suite 300, Bala Cynwyd, PA 19004.

5. *Nicolas and the Baby,* distributed by Educational Services, Division of American Journal of Nursing, 555 West 57th Street, New York, NY 10019.

6. *I'm a Little Jealous of That Baby,* distributed by Kids Corner, 2027 North Pejon, Colorado Springs, CO 80907.

7. "Week by Week, A Program to Prevent Pre-Term Birth, *Denver Post,* May 14, 1986.

8. *Guidelines on Early Discharge,* American Academy of Pediatrics.

9. "Early Discharge Following Low-Risk Delivery," *The Cybele Report* 5, no. 2 (Winter 1984).

Chapter 8
Other Alternatives

8

Alternative maternity program approaches that have evolved over the years started with the development of a birthing room. Often the hospital called this room or rooms an ABC, or alternative birth center. Other alternatives that have been developed are: LDR rooms, in-hospital midwifery centers, free-standing birthing centers.[1]

ALTERNATIVE BIRTH CENTERS (BIRTHING ROOMS)

Birthing rooms (or ABC rooms) were developed as a response to the emerging obstetrical consumer movement of the mid-1970s. Women were beginning to ask for options other than the traditional maternity approach to childbirth.

Often a room in the labor and delivery area, or sometimes on the postpartum unit, was designated and furnished as a birthing room. Wallpaper, plants, a rocking chair, and a birthing bed or double bed were provided; and the staff thought they had created alternatives for women. Frequently, the rooms were very small, located in out-of-the-way places, poorly lighted, and too full of furniture. However, this beginning approach to nontraditional care did indeed meet the identified needs of families at that time.[2]

Policies and procedures were revised by hospital staff, primarily nurses and physicians, for appropriate patient utilization of the room. Generally, very strict criteria were imposed for delivery in these rooms. Only very low-risk patients were determined to be appropriate to labor and deliver in the birthing room.

Advantages

Some hospital rules and regulations could be bypassed, providing for greater family involvement. The hospital was viewed by women consumers as being progressive and supportive.

Disadvantages

Because of the low-risk requirement, many women were disqualified from use of the room at the outset of labor. Others would begin the labor process in the ABC room, only to be moved to a traditional delivery room because they no longer met the criteria due to the possibility of complications. This angered many women, who thought they would get an alternative to the traditional delivery room, only to have it taken away. In many facilities, this occurred where birthing rooms and labor rooms were in the same location, were the same size, and essentially were no different except for decor, sign on the door, and the rules governing how the room could be used. Patients often questioned the need to be moved from one room to another when a complication occurred. Nursing staff sometimes acknowledged the patient's point, commenting that it did seem more reasonable to exchange door signs rather than move the patient.

Very frequently, the development of a birthing room created a complacent attitude among the staff, particularly staff nurses. The room, with its wallpaper and rocking chair, became more of a symbol that options for childbearing women were being provided. Too frequently, a few options were added, but care did not become more supportive of families. Instead, because the rules for using the room were so stringent, greater restrictions were possible.

LABOR, DELIVERY, AND RECOVERY (LDR) ROOMS

An LDR room is designed to allow a patient to labor, deliver, and recover in the same room within the traditional labor and delivery area. Following a short recovery period, the patient is then moved to a typical postpartum room. The LDR room is very large, often equivalent to the size of a delivery room. All high-tech equipment required for labor and delivery is kept in each room in an alcove that is screened from view until the equipment is needed. Overhead surgical lights are provided, sometimes permanently mounted and sometimes utilizing an elaborate track system by which the light can be pushed out of sight into the equipment area, when not in use. Basically an LDR room is a delivery room with a birthing bed, decorated with soft, comfortable, homey decor and furniture.

Advantages

Often physicians who are traditional in their style of care delivery will more readily accept an LDR room because it is viewed as less radical than a system such as single-room maternity care. The LDR room maintains the same labor and delivery nursing staff, and often the same style of care as in traditional labor and delivery rooms.

LDR rooms offer broader alternatives to families than is usually possible in a birthing room, mainly because of the larger size of the room. Family involvement and family-centered options desired by families are possible for the labor and delivery segments of childbirth in these rooms, if policies and procedures support them.

Disadvantages

Two systems of care are created within a labor and delivery area. Nurse staffing patterns remain the same, or in some cases, additional nursing staff have been required. Equipment needs are greater and more costly due to duplication of the high-tech equipment for each LDR room. Total square footage is often increased due to the size requirements of the rooms.

Although most transfers of the patient that occur in a traditional system are eliminated, the mother is still moved from the LDR room to her postpartum room. Most women, if given the choice, prefer not moving at all during the childbirth experience.

Many facilities manage their LDR rooms similar to birthing rooms, in that fairly strict criteria are established for a woman to qualify for delivery in an LDR room. Although LDR rooms can accommodate the needs for both low- and high-risk mothers, staff often are resistant to allowing this broad range of care.

LABOR, DELIVERY, RECOVERY, AND POSTPARTUM (LDRP) ROOMS

An LDRP room is similar to an LDR room with the added function of postpartum care. Here the patient may labor, deliver, recover, and receive postpartum care in the same room. Some health care providers believe this to be the same as single-room maternity care, but there are several important differences.

Instead of an entire system of childbearing rooms, as in single-room maternity care, most maternity care programs using LDRP rooms provide a number of rooms sized and equipped to handle care from admission to discharge, but maintain a traditional system around these rooms. In other words, a usual labor room approach is utilized for all patients not delivering in the LDRP rooms, and traditional postpartum rooms are used for most patients after delivery. Some consulting firms that advocate the use of LDRP rooms design each LDRP room with an equipment alcove much like an LDR room. They also recommend a small nursery be located near these rooms, on the assumption that twenty-four hour rooming-in will be common.

Hospitals that have built LDRP rooms use them primarily for short-stay or early discharge patients. This occurs for two reasons:

1. Because of staffing problems, it is more convenient to move patients to postpartum and provide longer-term care there.
2. Because of demand for the rooms, patients in the recovery or postpartum phase must be moved to postpartum to allow new patients to use the rooms for labor and delivery.

Advantages

Lower renovation costs are experienced than would be required to develop an entire system of childbearing rooms. However, because of individual room size and equipment needs, costs can be high.

Disadvantages

A patient desiring an LDRP room may not find it available if all rooms are occupied at the time of admission. Families wanting to stay in LDRP rooms until discharge may be asked to move to a traditional postpartum room at peak census times to make the LDRP room available for incoming patients in labor.

Equipment supplied in each LDRP room is more costly, due to duplication, than is experienced with a centralized equipment area.

Staffing both a traditional and an innovative care delivery system prevents staffing efficiencies and decreased operating costs.

A nursery sized for less-than-maximum occupancy has been found by functioning programs to be inadequate at peak census times. Many mothers do not desire twenty-four-hour rooming-in, especially during the nighttime hours. Mandating rooming-in, or appearing to do so, makes maternity patients feel they lack full freedom of choice with respect to their childbirth experience.

IN-HOSPITAL MIDWIFERY PROGRAMS

Several hospitals across the United States have developed midwifery programs. Reasons for a hospital pursuing a midwifery approach include economics, image change, and patient acquisition. In all cases midwives supplement physician care and can provide an added dimension to patient care.

Utilization of nurse midwives is often very attractive economically for a facility dealing with a high-risk, low-income, or indigent population. The workload volume and the geographical area often needed to be served can be overwhelming. Even with satellite prenatal clinics and other creative approaches to reach the indigent population, provision of care is extremely costly if only physician manpower is used. Nurse midwives, at a lower annual salary, can provide primary care and do low-risk deliveries with one or two physicians providing backup and any clinical care as needed.

Image change for the maternity program is another reason some hospitals have looked to in-hospital nurse midwifery programs. An example is the hospital that is perceived by people in the community to be very high-tech, high-risk, and strongly oriented to medical intervention in obstetrics. The addition of a midwifery program can be an effective way to change the image, and it provides many marketing possibilities.

In some markets, patient acquisition can be increased by nurse midwives. They have demonstrated the ability to attract patient populations that physicians have had difficulty attracting. Some women do prefer care by a nurse midwife and will seek it, if available. A large Hmong or other Southeast Asian population that for cultural reasons desires only women health care providers will be a heavy utilizer of this type of service. Also, an in-hospital midwifery program, with an attractive price package approach, can be very effective in attracting women who prefer a home delivery but decide to utilize the safer alternative of a hospital birth setting.[3]

Advantages

Nurse midwives in this country have successfully developed a high level of trust, conveying to patients the message that they truly offer women alternatives and control over their childbearing experience, including a low degree of medical intervention. Nurse midwifery programs can promote higher utilization of a department while generating lower costs.

Disadvantages

Many physicians are not interested in providing a nurse midwifery component to their obstetrics practice. Finding an obstetrician who will supervise the program and the practice of the nurse midwife is frequently difficult because of this. Nurse midwives, in many areas, also have had a great deal of difficulty obtaining hospital privileges to practice within a hospital setting.

Some women are very insistent on receiving only physician care and may avoid a physician practice or a hospital if they fear that they will not be given a choice between care by a nurse midwife and by the physician.

FREE-STANDING BIRTHING CENTERS

As the name implies, a free-standing birthing center is a maternity facility that is not physically connected to a hospital. It provides a first level of care, with a program designed to carefully screen for problems and triage women to other, more appropriate levels of care, as needed.

Two types of organizational relationships are utilized. In one, the free-standing facility maintains a relationship, administratively, clinically, and financially, with another facility, either a hospital or a physician practice. In the other, the free-standing facility is totally independent of any other facility. Many birthing centers of this latter type are developed and maintained by independent nurse midwives. A group of midwives will hire a physician to provide medical supervision and backup, while they provide all of the care. Frequently the nurse midwives in this particular type of program also obtain hospital privileges from an area facility in order to maintain continuity of care for the patient who requires hospitalization.[4]

One of the most successful free-standing facilities in the country is the San Dimas Birth Center in Bakersfield, California. The center is on the second floor of a two-story building owned and developed by five obstetricians. The physicians have their offices on the second floor, adjacent to the birth center. The first floor houses an outpatient surgical center, complete with capabilities to perform an emergency cesarean delivery if necessary. However, twenty-four-hour ambulance coverage is also available to move a mother or infant to the local hospital, approximately two miles away.

The center was designed using a single-room maternity care system, with nine childbearing rooms and other support functions aimed at making the parents' stay as comfortable and pleasant as possible. Laboring mothers are admitted directly to a childbearing room, where they labor, deliver and recover. Recovery time is based on demand for the room and individual patient need. However, all patients must be dismissed, either to home or to the hospital, within twenty-four hours. Follow-up care for patients delivering at the center is provided by the nursing staff.

Since its opening in November 1984, the center has been very successful. Projected volume goals for the first year were passed at approximately the seventh month of operation.

A variety of buildings and types of facilities are being used for free-standing birth centers. They range from utilization of a converted house, to vacated medical clinics, to a newly constructed center with many of the same medical provisions as a hospital.

Programmatic issues must be carefully researched and considered by any group considering development of a free-standing birthing center. Many states now have very rigorous rules and regulations for establishing these centers. Development of the program must ensure compliance with the laws for licensure. A major issue is that of transport policies and capabilities. Formal relationships must be established to ensure that a higher level of care can be provided quickly when needed. Another issue requiring careful procedure development is that of the continuing relationship with the primary care provider once transport to a hospital from a free-standing birthing center has occurred. Eligibility rules for admission to the center must be clear and carefully monitored.

Advantages

The owners have the autonomy to operate the center as they see fit, with the freedom to develop policies and procedures that support options and family-centered alternatives. Rules can be developed without having to convince other parties or seek cooperation, as is necessary in a hospital setting.

The consumer delivers in a pure alternative environment; one in which the childbearing woman and her partner can create their own desired experience.

Because of the screening process for admission to a free-standing center, the population must be low-risk. In addition, women choosing this type of environment tend to be healthier and more highly educated.

Disadvantages

Many centers, especially those owned by nurse midwives, are experiencing economic difficulties. They do not have the opportunities for other revenue bases, such as gynecological surgery, infertility diagnosis and treatment, or other procedures that generate revenue. Without these added services, a free-standing birthing center must do a very large volume to support the staff and meet the overhead required to operate the center.

Not every pregnant mother qualifies to deliver safely in a free-standing birthing center. Similar to the birthing room and other program options, this can be dissatisfying to women who plan for this approach to childbirth and then find it not available to them.

The safety of the medical backup systems, readily available in a hospital setting, often cannot be ensured in a free-standing birthing center. A medical complication to the mother or the infant, either during the labor process or following delivery, requires ambulance transfer to a hospital facility. Immediate intervention for a problem such as meconium aspiration in the neonate often cannot be aggressively managed on an immediate basis as it might be in a hospital.

Family-centered, client-driven maternity care can be delivered in almost any setting if the staff is philosophically committed to its value. The physical plant can be a barrier, or it can greatly facilitate and enhance the provision of individualized care. When changes are being considered, key staff members involved in the planning process must carefully explore alternative approaches to facility design. Market area analysis and program feasibility studies can promote a choice that will best carry their maternity care program into the future.

NOTES

1. M. Notelovitz, "The Single Unit Delivery System—A Safe Alternative to Home Deliveries," *American Journal of Obstetrics and Gynecology* 132 (1978): 887–894.

2. Susan McKay and Celeste R. Phillips, *Family-Centered Maternity Care* (Rockville: Aspen Publishers, Inc., 1984).

3. M.J. Kieffer, "The Birthing Room Concept at Phoenix Memorial Hospital, Part II: Consumer Satisfaction During One Year," *Journal of Obstetric, Gynecologic, and Neonatal Nursing,* May/June, 1980, pp. 151–159.

4. R.W. Lubis and E.K. Einst, "The Childbearing Cluster: An Alternative to Conventional Care," *Nursing Outlook* 26 (1978): 754–760.

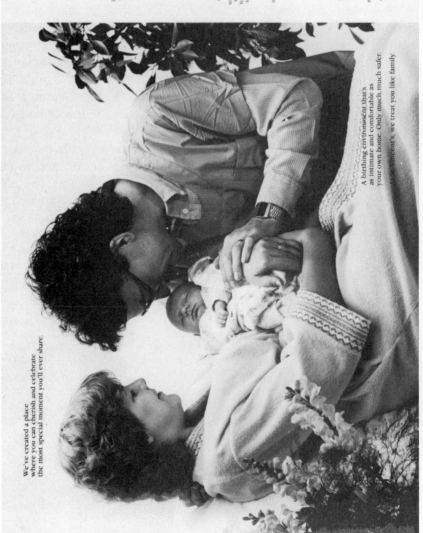

Case Study 1

St. Vincent Hospital and Medical Center, Portland, Oregon

The maternity program at St. Vincent Hospital and Medical Center is one of the more successful in the United States utilizing the LDR concept.

Facility Description

St. Vincent Hospital and Medical Center is a 451-bed not-for-profit facility owned and operated by the Sisters of Providence. St. Vincent is a tertiary care center located between the large urban population of Portland, Oregon and the growing communities of Washington County suburbs.

Motivating Factors for Change

Increasing maternity census in the early 1980s was pushing the facility to its maximum capacity of fourteen hundred births per year. At the same time, a goal was established to upgrade the obstetric service to a high Level II service. Pressed by these factors, the Maternal Child

Health Planning Committee recommended funding for a major remodeling of the obstetric unit.

Research Prior to Program Changes

Use of the "family birth room" had demonstrated obstetric patient interest in the concept of laboring and delivering in the same room, even though the room was not designed to accommodate any but the most low-risk patient. The only market research conducted was a preliminary needs assessment directed to all physicians providing maternity or pediatric care.

Planning Process

An ad hoc remodeling committee, chaired by the director of the OB/GYN department, was formed. Membership included three other obstetricians, three pediatricians, one family practice physician, an assistant director of nursing, the nursing unit manager, two nursing unit charge nurses, the hospital associate planner, and the assistant administrator of patient care services. Support was provided by architectural and medical planning consultants. The committee met eight times from May through December 1982 to fulfill its charge of recommending a feasible facility design for the third floor obstetrics unit. Actions taken by the group during these months included a medical staff survey, site trips to selected obstetric facilities, and meetings with medical and nursing staff.

Three alternative patient care concepts were reviewed from which the facility design options were chosen:

- traditional labor, delivery, and recovery rooms
- birthing rooms
- combination of labor, delivery, and recovery (LDR) rooms

The LDR concept was chosen to be the basis for the facility design because it was thought to blend the best of traditional and alternative approaches to childbirth. Each LDR room was planned to be large enough to provide sufficient work and equipment storage space for higher-risk patients, yet allow for a family orientation to the birth experience.

The ad hoc committee recommended to administration a remodeling plan that provided for, among other things, five LDR rooms, two high-risk labor rooms, and larger, improved nurseries. The recommended changes were expected to accommodate the projected growth in utilization to 1,935 deliveries by 1990.

Remodeling construction began in June 1983 and was completed in December. Two open houses were held in December; one for unit staff, physicians, office personnel and their families, and another for hospital staff. The following day the remodeled unit was opened for patient use. A public open house was delayed until February 1984, at which time the promotion centered on "A Special Birthday Party" for all babies born at the hospital since its opening in 1875.

Total Square Footage

Total square footage used by the maternity department prior to the change was approximately 18,000 square feet. No change in the amount of space was made when the initial remodeling was done. In 1984, the number of births increased by four hundred and thirty-eight. The obstetric unit expanded into another wing, thus occupying 28,600 square feet. Minor remodeling accompanied that move.

Project Budget

Project budget figures are unavailable.

Physician Profile

In 1983, St. Vincent had nineteen active OB/GYN physicians on staff. During 1983–84, three new physicians were added to the staff. Immediately following the opening of the BirthSuite LDRs, seven physicians who practice at two major competing hospitals began delivering the majority of their patients at St. Vincent.

Nurse Training Program

Nurses were introduced to the concept of LDR rooms and gained experience with family care during the remodeling, when semiprivate patient rooms were used as temporary LDRs. Because many nurses had previously cared for patients in the family birthing room, further education was not required.

Resisting Forces

The administrative staff requested information confirming that patient care in the LDR rooms was safe and efficient. Once provided, they were supportive of the project.

Nurses expressed concern that the new area would be too large and they would feel isolated from each other. Use of the temporary facility helped reduce the concern. Nursing staff had considerable input regarding the design of the unit from the very beginning. At each step of the design, a floor plan was made available to nursing and physician staff for their comments. All comments and concerns were addressed.

A number of physicians were included on the ad hoc remodeling committee. They represented their peers very well. All physicians were kept informed of the unit design plans as they developed. Their input was solicited and any concerns expressed were addressed.

Factors Influencing Success

The obstetric unit manager took temporary leave from her position and assumed the role of project coordinator, working closely with the designers, planners, physicians, nursing staff, and hospital construction coordinator. She helped maintain the excellent communication necessary to make the project successful. Obstetricians, nurses, and administrative staff formed a subcommittee that met regularly to solve problems throughout the first year of operation.

The physicians who were on the ad hoc remodeling committee communicated well with their peers. Physicians recognized consumer demand for the BirthSuite LDR concept and reacted favorably. Physicians are never denied the option of using the traditional delivery rooms for their patients. All options remain open.

St. Vincent initiated a strong marketing effort with the opening of the BirthSuite LDRs, including a TV spot and print advertising in several local publications. Women reacted positively and word spread quickly in the community.

Deliveries and FTEs

Deliveries

Calendar Year	Number of Deliveries
1981	1,420
1982	1,439
1983	1,541
1984	2,202
1985	2,332
Projected 1986	2,215

FTEs (Productive/Direct)

Calendar Year	Number of FTEs
1981	40.4
1982	39.1
1983	41.2
1984	46.7–54.3
1985	59.6
1986	52.5

Retrospective Decision Evaluation

It would have been more cost effective to build all the needed BirthSuite LDRs initially. Had market research been able to predict the dramatic rise in the birth census at St. Vincent, the entire third floor could have been dedicated to obstetric service, avoiding some of the continual remodeling that has taken place since 1984.

It would have been very helpful to have built a mock-up of a BirthSuite LDR prior to construction in order to test equipment placement and traffic flow. The test would have demonstrated the need for just a few more feet of space at the foot of the bed. Also, the nursing station areas were built too small for comfort and efficient organization. A mock-up of the nurses' station would have shown a need for more attention to traffic flow and efficiency.

Goal Achievement

The identified functional goals have been met, with the exception of accommodating growth through 1990. The number of rooms was correct for the projected number of patients (2,000). What was not expected was the 43 percent increase in births within the first six months of opening the BirthSuite LDRs. A sixth BirthSuite LDR was finished and put into service in June 1984.

Other goals achieved include:

- projection of an image to the patient and visitor of a nurturing, cheerful, and noninstitutional environment
- accomplishment of the design in a cost-effective manner, while conveying a subtle elegance
- creation of cost-effective staffing economics when possible
- maintenance of a competitive price structure in the community

Chapter 9
Factors To Consider

9

Planning for innovative maternity care changes requires a comprehensive, in-depth approach. In addition to the many issues already discussed, the factors that must be weighed and considered include regulatory requirements, norms of the local community population, and liability. Each facility and community will have subtle variations from a program in another location that it may be attempting to copy. These variations rarely will mean the difference between implementing or not implementing program changes, but early awareness will aid appropriate problem solving and planning. Recognizing the differences will prevent costly and often time-delaying last minute surprises, with program elements better targeted for maximum success.

STATE REGULATIONS

Many of the department of health regulations for maternity care in states across the country are antiquated and have not been updated to reflect the changes more progressive care requires. They represent the heavily restrictive surgical model of maternity care favored decades ago. Innovative maternity care that treats childbirth as a nonmedical family event does not fit within these old rules and regulations.

The department of health in each state is responsible to the citizens of the state to protect their interests regarding health care issues. It must carefully evaluate deviations and requests to change existing regulations to ensure continuing safety to consumers as they utilize health care institutions. The caution exercised by health department officials in adopting new concepts needs to be understood and respected.

Hospital staff, often anticipating an adversarial relationship with the state office, can create barriers to change and prevent positive outcomes. On the other hand, if hospital staff adopt an understanding and respectful approach, the door for effective communication will remain open. Efforts to build positive relationships in all interactions between health department offices and hospital staff promote collaboration and offer the best possible chance to revise and update state rules and regulations for maternity care in hospitals.

Health department regulations for maternity care have been changed in the past several years to accommodate the use of birthing rooms. However, these changes have been minimal. They merely allow labor and delivery in one or two rooms as an alternative to traditional care, while maintaining all of the restrictive requirements for the surrounding obstetrical unit.

As hospitals contemplate the major changes in patient care brought about with implementation of LDRs, LDRPs, and single-room maternity care, the unchanged regulations for obstetrics departments create major difficulties. When nontraditional maternity program changes are being planned, hospital staff should initiate dialogue with health department officials very early in the planning process. Hospital staff must be prepared to assist the health department staff to understand the concepts being proposed.

Proposed changes must be carefully outlined in detail, describing how the new system will work compared to a traditional obstetrical department. Hospital staff will need to critically evaluate regulations that present a conflict and research the rationale for the original establishment of the regulation. Compilation of data from current knowledge and experience will be useful in negotiating changes with health department staff. Often a consultant in maternity care design will be able to assist with data preparation and the rationale for change.

Facilities that have completed the change process have identified several disparities between existing health department regulations and the methods of providing progressive, family-centered maternity care. Some of the regulations causing disparities are:

- scrub sink requirements
- traditional delivery room air exchange requirements applied to LDR rooms or childbearing rooms
- requirements for number of labor rooms or delivery rooms per number of maternity beds that are reasonable only if all births occur in the traditional delivery area
- requirements for an examination room within the newborn nursery space, even though hospital staff use the existing room solely for storage
- requirements for formula rooms, even though formula is no longer prepared
- restrictions forbidding children of a new mother from visiting in the mother's room
- restrictions forbidding siblings of a new baby from holding or touching their new brother or sister
- specific restrictions regarding number of visitors or family allowed to visit a patient in labor or participate in the delivery event
- constraints on maximum allowable square footage (often quite limited) for private patient rooms

Methods for resolving disparities, once identified, vary depending on the specific regulation in question. For example, often in maternity unit redesign, formula room space is utilized for other functions. Challenging a formula room requirement may be effectively done by preparing a written document requesting a waiver to the regulation. Hospital staff working on the project will need to explain the previous function of a formula room and clearly describe how formula is presently processed and stored. Explanations of how the space can be better utilized to meet current program demands should be well developed and written out.

The question of air exchange requirements may require a different process to reach resolution. Traditional delivery rooms must meet the same ventilation requirements as operating rooms. The regulations are primarily aimed at promoting surgical asepsis. While this surgical environment is required for cesarean deliveries, recent experience indicates it is not necessary for vaginal births. In recent years, delivery of thousands of babies in birthing rooms, many of which are converted postpartum or labor rooms, has not demonstrated an increase in infections. Furthermore, to require the level of delivery room air exchange and the related mechanical capabilities for LDRs, LDRPs and childbearing rooms often is cost prohibitive. Steps that have been taken by facilities to effectively work with state health departments to resolve this issue include the following:

- Initiate verbal dialogue with a state health department representative for information sharing.
- Explain the facility's interest in program change and express the desire to problem solve collaboratively.
- Determine the posture of the state health department staff toward innovative or nontraditional change.
- Identify activity in the same programmatic area that is occurring with other facilities in the state. (This may be difficult to do in today's competitive environment.)
- Identify the capabilities of the mechanical/ventilating system serving the maternity space to be utilized.
- Elicit assistance from facilities in other states that have confronted these issues.
- Call consultants specializing in innovative maternity care design for assistance or advice.
- Develop a position paper for the state health department describing plans for program change, requesting waiver or outright change in the regulation, providing factual data regarding mechanical capabilities, and providing detailed rationale supporting the request. Since consumer safety, control of infection, and cost effectiveness are priorities of any department of health, the rationale must be strong in these areas.
- Encourage health department representatives to talk with their peers in other states who have been involved in this issue.

Provide the representatives with the names and phone numbers of contacts in other states where changes have been made.

- Arrange a face-to-face meeting with health department members and key hospital, medical, and nursing staff to discuss the issues.
- Identify further follow-up that may be required to reach resolution.

Any suggestion of a need to clarify outcome expectations or to negotiate with regulatory agencies requires early identification and action to achieve positive results. Health departments move slowly; a planned process of problem identification and establishment of mutual goals for resolution helps all concerned.

COMMUNITY NORMS

To achieve maximum success in the marketplace, the unique qualities, behaviors, and needs of a given community must be recognized and understood. Special components of the maternity care program tailored to the community will increase patient acquisition potential and positive perceptions about the program.

A comprehensive market survey provides data regarding the norms of each community. Periodic updating of marketplace behavior, perceptions, and needs of consumers is as important as the initial survey. Many marketing experts believe data more than six months old are no longer valid for program guidance in today's rapidly changing health care environment. Each change by a community health care provider and the resulting alteration of consumer behavior creates different responses and perceptions. Today the challenge for health care providers is not only to create a responsive client-driven program, but to continue to make appropriate adjustments as client needs and wishes change.

Some of the community variations that need to be considered in the design and marketing of maternity care services include the following:

- The use of analgesia/anesthesia versus nonmedicated natural childbirth varies greatly from city to city or one part of the country to another.
- The availability of double beds for postpartum families is very important in one area, but elicits no consumer interest whatsoever in another.
- The role and perception of the family physician versus the role the obstetrician in the practice of obstetrics varies greatly.
- The shift of control over hospital policy and program decisions from physicians to hospital administrative leaders is at a different level in each facility.
- The degree of assertiveness with which women are demanding services is variable. A market survey conducted in a northeastern state showed women to be very outspoken with their physicians; the same survey conducted in a southern city indicated women there were more willing to acquiesce to the doctor.
- Health care advertising is viewed in some areas as appropriate and expected; in other areas, even subtle promotion is not accepted.
- Consumer preference in hospital and patient room decor is regional. A down-home, country, frilly interior decor is the clear choice in some locations, as opposed to the more frequent preference for a contemporary, sophisticated, upscale appearance.

Particular community ethnic groups and cultures may require special consideration. Factors requiring attention are:

- *Religion.* Concentrations of any of the following religious groups (Catholic, Jewish, Mennonite, and Adventist, among others) require careful responses and adaptations to different work ethics, family planning practices, holiday and Sabbath observations, unique dietary expectations, and community visiting hour expectations.
- *Geographical origin.* A service area population that has significant numbers of Chicanos, Puerto Ricans, or Asian minorities,

including seasonal influxes of migrant workers, requires program components responsive to cultural differences. Bilingual program staff may be required or specific approaches to prenatal and postdelivery care may be necessary to motivate patients to participate in appropriate care.

- *Age mix.* A large teenage pregnancy population may require special locations and specific content for prenatal classes. A school system that responds to the students' needs for sex education, birth control counseling, and childcare for teenage mothers will require a different program approach than a school system that may address these issues less vigorously.

- *Rural-urban and white collar–blue collar mix.* Staff understanding of the subtle differences in the needs of these groups will encourage greater participation and involvement during pregnancy and childbirth. Blue collar workers are more likely to work evening or night shifts, while rural families may work all daylight hours during the summer months. Time and intensity of family involvement of both blue collar and rural families will be different from that of white collar families. The more completely nursing staff understand the differences in lifestyles and work ethics of the different groups, the more effectively they will be able to anticipate and respond to patients' needs.

- *Low-income and indigent population.* Decentralized, off-site prenatal and parenting classes may help meet the needs of a highly indigent population, for whom transportation to a central location is often a problem.

  Recognizing that a maternity stay in a well-decorated, comfortable family room provides a higher standard of living than many indigent patients possess will help staff anticipate the desire by some patients for a longer length of stay and to be "taken care of" by the nursing staff. Methods to encourage self-care should be discussed and formulated by the nursing staff.

LIABILITY

Perhaps the most urgent issue in all discussions of current programming and proposed changes is that of liability. Health care providers are "caught in the crunch." Consumers are demanding more options, involvement, and control. Third party payors are influencing treatment methods and length of stay by payment denial. Bottom line issues are becoming more critical while malpractice claims in obstetrics against hospitals and physicians are increasing at an alarming rate. Any program change being considered must be critically evaluated for its ability to meet the challenge of legal scrutiny.

The number of obstetricians no longer providing obstetrical care or contemplating this action is of great concern and poses a potential problem for both maternity consumers and hospitals. The same malpractice crisis often creates difficulties for hospitals attempting to recruit new physicians to practice obstetrics, especially in states where malpractice insurance premiums are highest. As the number of physicians delivering babies diminishes and affects market share, hospitals are looking for ways to assist attending medical staff with the high insurance costs.

A hospital must provide safe care at all times to all patients. This is increasingly difficult as financial issues become more critical. Finding the balance of cost effective maternity care without jeopardizing the safety and quality of care to either mother or infant is a serious challenge facing every administrator and hospital board member.

Safe care in the eyes of the law must be consistent with the standards of care. Standards of care can be elusive and are continually changing. Until only recently, care in one hospital was measured against local standards of care in the surrounding hospitals. Today, however, national standards are used as the yardstick for measuring acceptable care in any hospital. Simply stated, the standard of care is that care which a jury of peers in the same field of expertise will judge as reasonable and prudent at a specific point in time.

When planning maternity program changes, the rationale for each specific element of change must be scrutinized for its ability to meet a legal test. Implementing innovative maternity care need not compromise the acceptable standard of care. To the contrary, it should enhance it. Evaluating and planning all aspects of care, response times, and facility and equipment requirements with regard to potential liability is essential, and will be useful to the staff. Regulatory bodies will expect thoroughly prepared answers to their questions. Physicians and nurses working in the unit need reassurance that their liability risk is not increased. Hospital administrators and board members expect recommendations for program change to be sound and in the best interest of the hospital and its public.

A decrease in liability exposure is being demonstrated by innovative programs. Several factors contribute to this. A major factor creating greater safety for mother and infant involves the use of the same room and the same bed throughout the labor and birth process. The traditional practice of moving the mother from bed to bed and room to room while in the active and transitional phases of labor creates significant potential for accidents. Another factor in decreasing liability exposure is utilization of the cross-trained perinatal nurse. This professional is more highly skilled than the traditional obstetrical nurse, and the quality of nursing assessment, teaching, and care in all stages of the birth process has been demonstrated to be higher.[1]

Perhaps the most positive and significant contribution to reduce the litigious climate is the increased involvement of the patient, her partner, and family in the birth event, with the resulting high level of informed consent being demonstrated.

In years past, choosing a physician meant agreeing to accept the physician's choice of regimen; admission to a hospital meant accepting the hospital's routines and procedures. This is no longer true. People expect to be informed and consulted rather than simply to obey the decisions of physicians.[2] Informed consent is active, shared decision making between the provider and the patient. This process of decision making is based upon mutual respect and participation.[3]

Early consumer pressures to include fathers in the birth process by allowing his presence in the delivery room raised many fears that this action would trigger more lawsuits. The paranoia became worse when the father wanted to photograph the event. These fears have long been proven to be unfounded.[4]

The same phenomenon of heightened fears among health care providers is witnessed when family participation is promoted, allowing patient and partner to be actively involved throughout the entire childbearing process. Often during early planning for maternity program change, fears are expressed, especially by physicians, that by allowing the laboring woman and her partner to participate in decisions for the birth event, the hospital will create greater legal risk. This fear has not materialized. As the medical and nursing staffs work in partnership with the family, ongoing informed consent occurs. The continual sharing of information and decision making helps parents understand and accept problems when they occur. Conversely, forced physical exclusion of the partner when problems develop and limited sharing of factual information often cause fantasies of happenings worse than in fact do occur. The resulting anger, anxiety, and frustration are focused on the health care provider, and legal actions too often follow.

It is too early in the era of innovative, nontraditional maternity care to have long-term documented litigation data. However, current experience indicates that the partnership approach to childbirth reduces the risk of malpractice claims. Active participation of the parents must be coupled with open sharing of medical information about the progress of birth. Discussion of potential outcomes to mother and infant of available treatment options will help parents accept less-than-perfect outcomes without blaming the physician and/or the hospital staff. Only through time and experience with innovative family-centered maternity care programs will the effects on the malpractice scene be known.

NOTES

1. Linda Chagnon and Beverly Easterwood, "Managing the Risks of Obstetrical Nursing," *Maternal Child Nursing* 11 (1986): 303–310.

2. Mary Cipriano Silva and Peggy Lee Zeccolo, "Informed Consent: The Right To Know and the Right To Choose," *Nursing Management* 17 (1986): 18–19.

3. President's Commission for the Study of Ethical Problems in Medicine and Biomedical and Behavioral Research, *Making Health Care Decisions: The Ethical and Legal Implications of Informed Consent in the Patient-Practitioner Relationship, Vol. 1* (Washington D.C.: U.S. Government Printing Office, October 1982).

4. Margarete Sandelowski, "The Politics of Parenthood," *Maternal Child Nursing* 11 (1986): 235–238.

Part III

Innovative Women's Services: Before and After Childbearing

The Importance of Building a Market through Women's Health Care

10

Building a market through the delivery of women's health care programs has suddenly captured the interest of every hospital administrator in the country. In an effort to keep pace with trends, many hospitals are implementing programs without full recognition and understanding of the benefits or potential pitfalls of these programs. This is reflected in the superficial and fragmented approach in which many programs have been developed and are being operated.

A far more serious approach to women's health care services is warranted. The method of delivering health care must change to accommodate the changes occurring in society. Statistics indicate that there are now eight million more women than men.[1] As indicated in previous chapters, women have a different orientation to health care than do men. For example, women are more interested in having information about health care in general and about the options for health care provision. Women show a greater interest than men in seeking and adopting preventive health measures. Women are interested in physical, social, and psychological health, while men seem to be only interested in physical well-being.

Just like the changes that have occurred in maternity care, it is unlikely that the changes occurring in women's health care will reverse themselves in the near future. Hospitals that survive and do well in the current health care arena will be those that take advantage of the opportunities afforded by changes in society. Survival also depends on moving quickly to position the hospital in the marketplace. However, program implementation must be done with sensitivity and careful planning to avoid the superficial, fragmented approach mentioned earlier.

WHY DEVELOP PROGRAMS FOR WOMEN

One of the major reasons for developing women's programs and services is to create or enhance a hospital's image with women. Creating such an image will distinguish the hospital from its competition, highlighting it as an institution that provides more than traditional acute care services. Programs and services for women also tend to create an image of the hospital that is more compatible with the interest women have shown for preventive health care programs versus acute hospital services.

An equally important motivation for developing women's health care programs and services is the "spinoff" to all other programs and services in the hospital. This spinoff effect has both short- and long-term ramifications. In the short-term, a premenstrual syndrome (PMS) program, for example, can generate additional revenue through diagnostic lab and x-ray work. Research has shown that the average PMS patient presents with twenty-eight different symptoms; thus ancillary services become an important tool in the initial work-up of these patients.[2]

Over a longer period of time, women's health care services can serve to initiate the development of an ongoing relationship between a woman, her family, and the hospital. If the woman becomes associated with the hospital through an outpatient women's center, she is more likely to refer members of her family to that facility should the need arise.

Another benefit that is derived from the development of women's health care services is the ability to attract and retain highly qualified physicians and nonphysician specialists, who may also draw new or greater numbers of women to the hospital. An outpatient women's center that is structured to augment and support the private physician practitioner can be a major source of patient referrals as well.

CHARACTERISTICS OF TODAY'S WOMAN

In order to successfully accomplish the goals possible through the development of women's health care programs and services, it is necessary to design programs and services that reflect the needs and desires of today's woman. Today's women are:

- better educated
- skeptical and discriminating
- nonconforming
- becoming intolerant of the inconveniences of traditional health care delivery

Today's women want:

- marriage later
- fewer children
- comprehensive technical information about health care problems
- participation in health care decisions
- quality health care at a reasonable cost
- to be more than a wife and mother

Many providers make the mistake of not realizing that women are changing. This fallacy can lead to the treatment, philosophically and clinically, of women in accordance with old stereotypes. One women's health care consultant observed, "These stereotypes can be dangerous even when they linger only subconsciously in the mind of health care providers and planners."[3] This consultant also states that the benefit of implementing programs and services that women want can be negated by the manner in which they are delivered. An outstanding array of services will attract women to the hospital, but inefficiency, rudeness, or insensitivity by the staff will keep women from returning.

The following statistics provide a general profile of women in the 1980s. These statistics reflect the changes occurring among women and will assist the program planner to better know and understand what is needed. It should be noted that these statistics provide only a general description. Comprehensive market analysis will be needed to determine the special characteristics of individual target markets in a particular hospital's service area.

Women and Age[4]

- The population as a whole is aging:
  - —In 1970, 9.8 percent (20 million) were sixty-five years of age or older.
  - —In 1980, 11.3 percent (26 million) were sixty-five years of age or older.
  - —In 2000, 13.1 percent (35 million) will be sixty-five years of age or older.
- The older population is getting older:
  - —In 1980, 39 percent of the elderly were seventy-five years of age or older.
  - —In 2000, 50 percent of the elderly will be seventy-five years of age or older.
- Elderly women outnumber elderly men three to two:
  - —Life expectancy for females is 78.2 years and 70.9 years for males.
  - —There are eighty men for every one hundred women age sixty-five to sixty-nine.
  - —There are forty-two men for every one hundred women age eighty-five and older.

Women and Marriage

- Although 90 percent of American young people expect to marry, the number of marriages is declining:
  - —The rate of 10.5 per 1000 population (2,487,000 marriages) in 1984 is the lowest since 1979.[5]
- Today, many couples live together without marrying. In 1986, almost 2 million unmarried couples are living together, nearly four times as many as in 1970.[6]

- Many women are marrying later in life or not marrying at all:
  —In 1970, thirty-six percent of women between the ages of twenty and twenty-four were not married. In 1986, fifty-six percent of women in this age group are not married.[7]
  —College-educated women marry even less frequently. At age thirty, white college-educated women have a twenty percent probability of marriage. At age thirty-five, this probability drops to 5.4 percent. At age forty, the probability of marriage is 1.3 percent. Probabilities are even lower for black college-educated women age thirty and older.[8]

- Many of those who marry have been married previously:
  —Forty-five percent of all new marriages are remarriages.[9]
  —Three out of four divorced women remarry.[10]

- After a decline in the number of divorces in the early 1980s, divorces are again increasing.[11] If this trend continues, one-half of marriages today will end in divorce.

- The likelihood of divorce varies with age and circumstances:
  —Highly educated women making over $20,000 per year have a divorce rate four times higher than that of the general population.[12]
  —Ninety-five percent of couples over fifty years of age stay married, so divorce is more likely to occur to those who are younger.[13]

- Divorce takes its economic toll most dramatically on women:
  —Following divorce, women experience a seventy-three percent decline in their standard of living.[14]
  —Following divorce, men experience a forty-two percent increase in their standard of living.[15]

- Divorce often creates increased responsibilities for women:
  —Ninety percent of children of divorced parents live with their mothers. Over one-half of these children have had no contact with their father in the last year.[16]
  —Forty-two percent of children in divorced families receive no child support; more than one-half of all fathers do not pay full child support.[17]

- A significant and growing number of people live alone:
  - —The number of those living alone almost doubled between 1970 and 1985 (10.9 million in 1970 and 20.6 million in 1985).[18]
  - —Almost one in four households (23.1 percent) in 1985 was a single-person household.[19]
  - —The median age of those living alone differs by sex: 41.4 years for men; 65.5 years for women.[20]

Women and Children

- The fertility rate (live births per 1000) for women age fifteen through forty-four has declined in this decade (from 71.1 per 1000 in 1980 to 65.8 per 1000 in the year ending June 30, 1984).[21]
- However, because of the large number of women in the child-bearing years, the number of births continues to increase each year. The number of births in 1984 (3.7 million) increased by two percent over 1983 births.[22]
- But not all women are choosing to have children today:
  - —In 1960, only thirteen percent of married women between ages twenty-five and twenty-nine were childless. In 1985, twenty-nine percent of this age group were childless.[23]
  - —Today, one out of four ever-married women (nearly 3.3 million) between the ages of twenty-five and thirty-four years of age has never had a child, compared to one out of ten women in 1960 (see Figure 10–1).[24]
- The increasing age of mothers at first birth also contributes to a yearly increase in numbers of births:
  - —In 1950, eighty percent of women had a child before age thirty. In 1986, this percentage had dropped to sixty percent for women thirty years of age or younger.[25]
  - —The fertility rate is rising for women age thirty through thirty-four: from sixty live births per 1000 in 1980 to 72.2 per 1000 in 1984.[26]
- By 1990, as the baby boom generation moves into middle age, the number of women in the childbearing years is projected to decrease by twenty-five percent.[27] If fertility rates stabilize or continue to decline, the number of births should also decline.

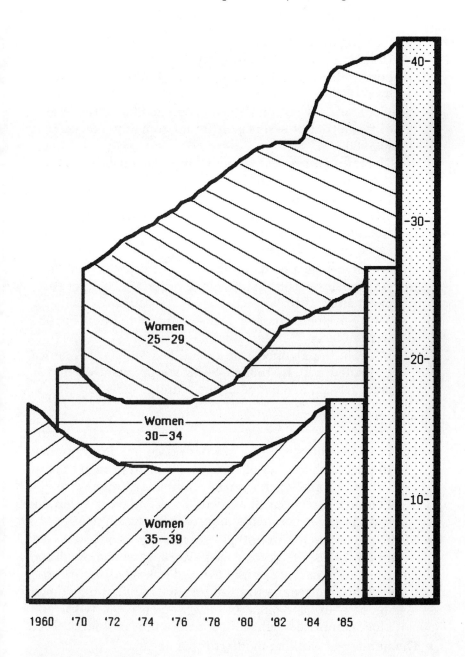

Figure 10–1 Increase in Childlessness (in Percent)

Source: National Center for Health Statistics, Census Bureau.

- Childbearing by unmarried women is growing:
    —Unmarried women had twenty-one percent of all babies born in 1984, an all time high and a four percent increase over 1983.
    —Women age twenty and older accounted for sixty-five percent of all out-of-wedlock births, up from fifty-nine percent in 1980.[28]
    —The rate of birth among single white women has increased three times since 1960.[29]
    —In 1984, almost twenty-five percent of households with children under age eighteen were headed by an unmarried woman. This percentage is expected to increase to fifty-seven percent by 1990.[30]
- The rate of teenage pregnancy is declining. In 1984, the rate of births to females age fifteen through nineteen was 50.9 per 1000, the lowest since 1940.[31]
    —Thirty-five percent of all births to unwed mothers in 1984 were to teens.[32]
    —In 1985, the Planned Parenthood Federation of America estimated that 1.1 million teens are pregnant each year and fourteen percent of all births are to teens.

Women and Work

- The number and percentage of working women is increasing:
    —In the fourth quarter of 1985, 51.5 million women were in the work force, up 2.8 percent from the previous year.[33]
    —Fifty-five percent of all women age 16 and older are in the work force, as compared to forty-four percent in 1970.[34]
- Older women are in the workplace in greater numbers:
    —In the 1980s, the percentage of working women in all age categories, except age fifty-five and older, has increased.
    —In 1970, fourteen percent of the labor force were women age forty-five and older. In 1982, women age forty-five and older comprised eighteen percent of the labor force.[35]
- The number of working mothers is significant:
    —Twenty million women with children under age eighteen work outside the home.[36]

—Twenty-five million children have mothers who work outside the home.[37]

—In 1970, 32.3 percent of the women with children under the age of six were working. In 1984, the percentage rose to 52.1 percent (4.2 million). By 1990, the number is predicted to reach sixty-four percent.[38]

—Each child with working parents may require two or three child care arrangements.[39]

- Ten million women are sole supporters of their families.[40]

Women and Poverty

- Thirteen million women (ten percent of all women) live in poverty. Of these, 8.8 million are Caucasian.[41]
- Forty-seven percent of single women live in poverty.[42]
- The number of poor people in families headed by women jumped twenty-five percent in the past four years.[43]
- If present trends continue, by 1990 one in every four children under age eighteen will be living in poverty and two-thirds of children with unmarried mothers will live in poverty.[44]

Between June 1985 and October 1986, Dearing & Associates collected public opinion information from 8,052 women across the country. Data were gathered on their response to innovations in health care services for women and on the factors that influence their choice of health care providers. It should be noted that not all women responded to every question. Appendix 10–A describes the methodology of and findings from the opinion surveys. Following is a summary of key points.

- Women were questioned about how they selected a hospital. They indicated that the following factors most frequently influenced their choice:
    —Their physician has hospital privileges at the hospital chosen.
    —The hospital is staffed by professional, caring nurses.
    —The hospital has attractive, modern facilities and equipment.

- The most important criteria for the selection of a physician by those surveyed on this issue were:
    —competency
    —personality
    —ability to communicate well
- When asked if they would switch physicians if they could not relate to their physician, 89.1 percent (4,038) of those questioned said that they would change doctors.
- Ninety-four percent (4,377) of all of those surveyed on this issue indicated that hospitals should advertise services.
- Respondents in large numbers expressed a preference for innovative maternity care. 4,555 respondents chose single-room maternity care as described in Chapter 5; and 2,596 of these women indicated they would switch physicians in order to have single-room maternity care.
- Respondents in large numbers also expressed an interest in having outpatient women's centers available in their area. At least three-fourths of all women surveyed—from all parts of the country—favored the establishment of such a center in their community. However, many more women would like to have a center with a wide array of available services than would use such services.
- There is a clear preference for outpatient services to be offered on weekday evenings and Saturday morning. Most women prefer that these services be located on a hospital campus.

WHAT WOMEN WANT TO BUY

There are two components that specifically constitute what women are seeking from health care providers. These components are:

1. An array of services that address physical, psychosocial, and emotional needs.
2. A method of service delivery that is responsive to each woman as an individual.

Special services oriented to a particular market segment and designed to provide preventive as well as acute care are the types of services women want and are willing to buy. An example of these services: a special inpatient unit providing the medical-surgical patient highly individualized care, with special diets and amenities; an exercise class structured for the professional woman offered at 6:30 A.M.; a support-therapy group for the older woman who has primary responsibility for an ailing relative.

Because women want greater participation in the decision making process involving their health care needs, the manner in which the services or programs are offered clearly affects their response and willingness to buy. As more and more hospitals enter the women's health care market, greater emphasis will need to be placed on thoughtful, precise planning and implementation to avoid superficial, fragmented results.

COMPONENTS AFFECTING SERVICE DELIVERY

Key components affecting service delivery fall into two categories. The first category centers on the functional and physical aspects with which the service is delivered. The second category focuses on the attitude and manner with which the service is delivered.

Category I: Convenience

Convenience will vary significantly with each market segment. Among the factors to be considered:

- comfortable, pleasant environment
- location
- hours of service
- timeliness of appointment
- scheduling of appointment
- seeing the patient on time
- safe and close parking
- other services:

—childcare
—transportation
—parking fee compensation
—handicap facilities
—reading materials in large print for the sight-impaired

Category II: Responsive Approach

This requires staff training to tune out stereotypes and tune in to the uniqueness of each individual patient.

- personal attention
    —staff who are willing to listen and respond
    —smiling, friendly, positive staff
    —staff who anticipate and offer small, helpful favors (calling a taxi, providing a telephone number for another resource)
- respectful manner
    —addressing patients by the name they prefer
    —ensuring privacy for all patients
- adequate staff and time to appropriately handle each patient's needs
- thoughtful, complete information taken and given

All of this can be summarized in one overriding tenet that must be the singular approach of every staff member:

IF YOU THINK THERE IS SOMETHING MORE IMPORTANT THAN
YOUR PATIENT, THINK AGAIN!

How These Characteristics Determine the Development and Delivery of Services

Once the general characteristics have been noted and assimilated with market specific information for an individual facility, it is necessary to translate the information into program and service design.

The importance of market specific information cannot be over-emphasized. Do not be lulled into thinking that all women in the 1980s are the same. While market research has demonstrated certain national trends, there are also various nuances or differences among women living in some communities and regions.

These differences have a significant impact on which program or service is offered, how it is delivered, and the manner and method chosen for marketing. One model, whether for service or marketing, will not work in every setting. All models must be modified and adapted for local variations. For example, a market analysis for a rural community hospital in Georgia revealed that a significant portion of the maternity care patient population were members of the Mennonite religion. Certain hospital policies were incompatible with the lifestyle of this group. Mennonites are farm people with a strong family orientation. The hospital's maternity care department did not permit visiting on Saturday mornings, which is historically the day these families come to town. The hospital was especially interested in attracting and pleasing this market segment. Yet, until the market study, hospital staff had failed to consider the special visitation needs of this group. Policies have been changed to promote flexible visitation privileges for all families and visitors to the hospital.

Some hospital staff have unthinkingly assumed they could lift an entire program and marketing plan not only from one state to another, but from a metropolitan area to a rural community. Often this is done in an effort to save money or produce results more quickly. It rarely works. Usually the effects are exactly the opposite: in the long-run, this type of program development and marketing will cost more and take longer.

NOTES

1. U.S. Bureau of Census, 1984.

2. William Keye, MD, "Product Line Development: A Case Study in Gynecological Care," Women's Health Care: A Profitable Product Line (Conference). Chicago, IL: April 14–15, 1986.

3. Sally J. Rynne, "Twelve Stereotypes That Can Sabotage Success." *Marketing Women's Health Care Newsletter,* Summer 1986.

4. U.S. Bureau of Census, 1984.

5. Department of Health and Human Services, Vital Statistics, 1985.
6. "ABC News Close-up: After the Sexual Revolution," aired July 30, 1986.
7. *Ibid.*
8. *Ibid.*
9. *Ibid.*
10. *Ibid.*
11. Portland (Oreg.) *The Oregonian,* January 4, 1986.
12. "ABC News Close-up: After the Sexual Revolution," aired July 30, 1986.
13. *Ibid.*
14. *Ibid.*
15. *Ibid.*
16. *Ibid.*
17. *Ibid.*
18. U.S. Bureau of Census, 1984.
19. *Ibid.*
20. *Ibid.*
21. *Ibid.*
22. National Center for Health Statistics, 1985.
23. "Three's a Crowd," *Newsweek,* September 1, 1986, p. 68.
24. *Ibid.*
25. "ABC News Close-up: After the Sexual Revolution," aired July 30, 1986.
26. U.S. Bureau of Census, 1984.
27. *Kiplinger Newsletter,* August, 1985.
28. National Center for Health Statistics, 1985.
29. "ABC News Close-up: After the Sexual Revolution," aired July 30, 1986.
30. *Ibid.*
31. National Center for Health Statistics, 1985.
32. *Ibid.*
33. U.S. Department of Labor, Bureau of Labor Statistics.
34. *Ibid.*
35. *Ibid.*
36. U.S. Bureau of Census, 1984.
37. *Ibid.*
38. *The Sacramento Bee,* August 26, 1985, Section C-1.
39. "ABC News Close-up: After the Sexual Revolution," aired July 30, 1986.
40. *Ibid.*

41. *Business Week,* January 28, 1985, p. 84.

42. "ABC News Close-up: After the Sexual Revolution," aired July 30, 1986.

43. *Business Week,* January 28, 1985, p. 84.

44. "ABC News Close-up: After the Sexual Revolution," aired July 30, 1986.

Summary of Public Opinion of Women Surveyed by Dearing & Associates between June 1985 and October 1986

Since June 1985, Dearing & Associates has been collecting public opinion data from women across the country regarding their response to innovations in health care services for women and the factors that influence their choice of health care providers. Public opinion was gathered from the following sources:

1. telephone surveys
2. focus groups
3. questionnaires completed by female patients of hospital clients of Dearing & Associates
4. questionnaires completed by female employees of hospital clients of Dearing & Associates

Methodology

It should be noted that not all women responded to every question. Percentages were computed on the number of women responding to each question.

The methodology for collecting data in each of these areas was as follows.

Telephone Surveys

Potential respondents were randomly selected from the most recent telephone directories for the service areas of hospitals with which the firm consulted between June 1985 and October 1986. Criteria for participation were that the respondent be a woman between the ages of eighteen to sixty, who was not employed by a health care organization or physician. Two to three attempts were made to contact each selected respondent.

A standard questionnaire was used to gather information from all respondents. Only women respondents forty years of age or less were asked questions regarding maternity care. All respondents were asked questions about women's health care (exclusive of maternity care). All respondents were contacted between 9:00 A.M. to 12:00 noon and 5:00 to 9:30 P.M. local time. A total of 3,095 respondents were interviewed by this method.

Written Questionnaires

A standard questionnaire, similar to the one used for telephone interviews, was completed by a representative number of female patients and female employees of client hospitals during the time period June 1985 to October 1986. Questionnaires were distributed by hospital employees and returned in sealed envelopes to Dearing & Associates for analysis.

The same questionnaire was completed by participants of focus groups conducted by Dearing & Associates. In most instances, focus group participants were recruited by local survey research organizations in accord with criteria established by Dearing & Associates to ensure a cross-section of ages, socioeconomic status, and place of residence. Participants who worked in health care or for advertising and public relations agencies were screened out. Participants were paid a modest incentive fee for their assistance.

Occasionally, a client organized a focus group composed of professional women and local opinion leaders among women in the community. These participants were included in the survey, although they did not always meet the criteria established for other focus groups. They were not compensated for their time.

A total of 4,957 women completed written questionnaires.

Women who participated in the surveys and focus groups lived in the following states: Arizona, California, Connecticut, Georgia, Kentucky, Massachusetts, Michigan, North Carolina, Ohio, Oregon, Pennsylvania, and Tennessee.

Findings

1. Those respondents who completed written questionnaires
    were asked to list the three factors they consider most impor-
    tant when choosing a hospital. A total of 4,903 women
    responded to this question. The three most frequently men-
    tioned factors are noted below in order of preference:

    - their physician's hospital privileges
    - professional, caring nurses
    - attractive, modern facilities and equipment

2. Written questionnaire respondents were also asked to note
    the most important criteria in their selection of a physician. A
    total of 4,945 women responded. Following is a listing in order
    of importance of factors considered in choosing a physician:

    - competency
    - personality
    - ability to communicate well

3. Questionnaire respondents were asked if they would switch
    physicians if they could not relate to their doctor. A total of
    89.1 percent (4,038) indicated they would find another physi-
    cian if this situation occurred. Many respondents indicated
    they had already taken such action.
4. These respondents were asked about their preference for
    semiprivate or private hospital rooms. A total of 69.9 percent
    (3,201) of all the respondents to written questionnaires pre-
    ferred private rooms, 24.9 percent (1,139) preferred semi-
    private rooms, and 5.2 percent (241) expressed no
    preference.
5. Questionnaire respondents were asked if hospitals should
    advertise. Ninety-four percent (4,377) answered Yes. Only six
    percent (279) of the women answered No to this question.

6. Respondents to both the telephone survey and the question-naire were asked their reaction to single-room maternity care, as described in Chapter 5. Eighty-nine percent (4,555) of respondents, including telephone respondents in the child-bearing years, indicated a preference for single-room mater-nity care if it was available in their community or nearby.

7. When asked if they would switch physicians to have single-room maternity care, 5,265 women responded. Of these, 49.3 percent (2,596) said they would switch physicians in order to have single-room maternity care.

8. A total of 78.7 percent (3,902) of all respondents to the written questionnaire preferred rooming-in as desired by the mother.

9. Of the written questionnaire respondents who answered the questionnaire on this issue, 94.6 percent (4,221) wanted the pediatrician to examine the baby in their room and talk with the mother about the examination.

10. A total of 5,754 women responded by telephone survey and written questionnaire to the question about preference for a reduced-fee, reduced-stay maternity care option. Of these, 55.8 percent (3,210) said they would choose a 24-hour re-duced-fee option if it were available.

11. In each community, over three-fourths of women surveyed by telephone and written questionnaires were interested in seeing an outpatient women's health center established in their community.

12. Those surveyed by telephone and written questionnaire ranked services they thought should be included in a women's health care center in the following order:

- breast examination   78.0% (5,885)
- PMS treatment   74.5% (5,623)
- menopause treatment   74.1% (5,590)
- special exercise program   68.5% (5,165)
- self-improvement classes   67.5% (5,095)
- special diet program   67.5% (5,090)
- laser GYN surgery   65.0% (4,903)
- substance abuse program   51.0% (3,851)

However, in response to the question "Which of these services would you use?" the positive responses were lower:

- breast examination — 60.2% (4,543)
- special exercise program — 48.4% (3,653)
- special diet program — 47.5% (3,583)
- self-improvement classes — 45.8% (3,458)
- laser GYN surgery — 42.7% (3,220)
- PMS treatment — 33.3% (2,514)
- substance abuse program — 23.9% (1,804)
- menopause treatment — 23.5% (1,775)

13. There was a clear preference for the center to offer services during the week in the evenings (43.4 percent, 3,834 responses). About 25 percent (2,163) of the responses indicated a preference for Saturday mornings.
14. Of those asked about the preferred location for a women's center, 25.3 percent (1,677) chose a site in an acute care hospital, 49.5 percent (3,283) preferred the center be located in a separate building on the hospital campus, and 24.9 percent (1,652) preferred an off-campus location.

Outpatient Services: The Women's Center

11

WHAT A WOMEN'S CENTER IS AND DOES

Very few outpatient women's health care centers exist today, especially ones that offer a comprehensive array of services and provide women's health care in a way that truly responds to the needs of women in the community it serves. Generally, there are three key reasons motivating a hospital to initiate such programs:

1. to provide additional services that fill an unmet need and generate new revenue for the hospital
2. to establish a vehicle for capturing the women's market by positioning the hospital positively with women
3. to increase the overall attractiveness of the hospital by creating a positive relationship in this one area

Purpose

The purpose of the women's health care center is to provide services that respond to the total needs of women: physical, psychosocial, and emotional. The programs and services are meant to augment and complement (not duplicate) the hospital's existing service base. Additionally, programs and services need to be structured to work in tandem with the attending medical staff, so as not to compete with them for the primary care market.

223

Philosophy

Many providers recognize the benefits of an outpatient women's health care center, but fail to capitalize fully on these benefits because of the manner in which services are delivered. The philosophy that guides program and service delivery is as important to the center's success as the array of programs and services offered. The appropriate philosophy for care delivery in an outpatient women's center has three basic principles:

1. Programs and services should promote an expanded definition of health that includes emotional and social as well as physical well-being.
2. Care should be delivered with respect for the dignity and individuality of each patient.
3. Patients should be encouraged to take an active role in creating and maintaining good health.

Many health care staff members do not adhere to this philosophy. Thus it will be necessary to carefully select and educate the clinical staff employed in the center. Clerical and support staff will also need to be oriented and trained to respond with the same philosophical approach.

Functions

The functions of an outpatient women's health care center emerge out of the purpose and the philosophy described above. The functions of a women's health care center are:

1. diagnosis and testing
2. education
3. support therapy
4. health promotion

To ensure that the center does not establish a competitive or adversarial relationship with the attending medical staff, treatment should be provided on a highly selective basis. The functions of the center are specifically designed to serve the private practitioner, as well as the woman patient, by providing support and assistance to better meet patient needs. There are some circumstances where provision of treatment is appropriate. For example:

1. Tertiary level or subspecialty programs not offered by private attendings, such as genetics counseling.
2. Programs or services in which the private physicians do not have interest or time to adequately provide care, such as PMS counseling.
3. Programs or services that require equipment too costly for the private physician to own, for example, CO_2 laser surgery.

Service Selection

Programs and services offered at the outpatient women's health care center can include existing or established services offered by the hospital, in conjunction with new programs and services that are developed. Often we find that hospitals overlook some of the services currently offered. Thus, it is necessary to inventory existing services to determine which ones are suitable for promotion through the women's center. Frequently the existing programs or services will need to be restructured and repackaged to make them consistent with the philosophy and image the center is promoting.

New programs or services need to be selected based upon the following criteria:

- community interest and potential for support
- market opportunity
- expertise of physicians
- support of attending medical staff
- existing services that are now part of other programs

Market area analysis is the mechanism for determining the degree and probable outcome of each criterion listed above. Two important points must be kept in the forefront of planning and development:

1. Researchers need to distinguish between what women want and what they will use. A significantly smaller number of women express willingness to use a service than the number of women indicating an interest in having the program available.
2. Program developers need to suspend preconceived notions and planning activities until the results of market research indicate which programs the public will support. In many situations, hospital staff develop and implement programs and services based solely on their perception of what women want and need. Market research conducted after program implementation frequently shows the existing programs to rank low in priority for use by the hospital's service area residents.

Other information gathered from market research will be useful in program and service design and development. The following factors should be explored through market research:

1. *Location of the center.* A center should be located on-campus if possible, to ensure visual connections with the hospital. In any case, it should be easily accessible to potential users.
2. *Hours of service.* Evening and weekend hours are essential. Special religious or cultural groups among target markets should be noted and their needs accommodated.
3. *Childcare.* A women's center can increase utilization if childcare services are provided.
4. *Payment alternatives.* Instituting a sliding pay scale and payment arrangements will increase utilization.

Establishing a Referral Base

A multifaceted referral base will need to be developed to support the outpatient women's health care center. There are three components necessary to develop an effective service base:

1. *The Physician Component*
   The success of any hospital-based women's health care center depends on physician support and participation. Many women, especially older women, still rely on a physician's

opinion or recommendation and will not use a center without their physician's support.

It is essential that physicians view the center as supportive of their practices. It is important to involve physicians in planning and development, service provision, and marketing.

Physicians must be educated to be well informed and knowledgeable of the center's philosophy and activities in order to feel comfortable and advocate its use to their patients.

An equitable referral system must be developed to ensure ongoing physician participation. The referral system needs to be established in such a way as to assure referral of new patients to all physicians participating in the center's activities.

2. *The Patient Component*

Many women will come to the center on their own. Thus the hospital needs to market the programs and services offered, directly to women as well as to physicians. Service design and the advertising/promotional campaign must be matched with women's needs, expectations, and values in order to gain their attention and support.

A system for handling women who come to the center without a physician referral must be established. This system must be sensitive to existing relationships the patient may have already established with a private physician.

3. *The Community Component*

Community-based organizations can be sources of patient referrals to a women's center. The hospital needs to develop relationships with these groups to assure their knowledge and understanding of the programs and services provided at the women's center.

Strategies for accomplishing this include joint programming, positions on advisory committees, frequent ongoing communication, and special discounts or programs offered to members or clients.

In order to be successful, the women's health care center will require a broad base of support, from both inside and outside the hospital. As noted above, physician support is essential. In addition, support is necessary from top management, hospital employees, and volunteers. Employees and volunteers constitute a good market segment for use of the center. They can also provide valuable assistance in promoting the center to family, friends, and community residents.

Establishment of an advisory committee composed of leaders among women in the community will serve as an excellent mechanism for gathering input and developing support for the center. The purpose of such a committee is to provide information, not to dictate policy or determine operational functions. The advisory committee membership can also include center staff, physician participants, and marketing and public relations staff.

Organizational Structure and Staffing

We have found that in order to ensure program effectiveness and coordination, it is best to organize the center as a product line, with a manager reporting to a member of the hospital's top management team. This manager can be responsible for all women's health care programs and services, both inpatient and outpatient. The position should be filled by a woman with strong management and public relations skills. Clinical expertise is less important than the abilities to organize, manage, motivate, and promote.

The center can be staffed mostly by nurse clinicians and allied health professionals. It is not necessary that all of the staff be women. Far more important is that all employees like women and share the philosophy upon which the center has been developed. Required physician manpower should be provided by the attending medical staff whenever possible.

Creating an Image

Exterior and interior decor, advertising, promotion, marketing, and signage must be coordinated to ensure a consistent and appealing image. In developing an image for the women's health care center, it is important to create one that is compatible with the hospital's overall image.

Again, knowledge of the market will be beneficial to determine the image the hospital wishes to put forth through the women's center. Certain colors and designs are more appealing to women and more likely to generate interest. The language of brochures, billboards, and other promotional materials must be carefully worded to convey the image in a way that will cause women to respond.

To a significant degree, the staff of any organization influences its image, whether positively or negatively. The staff in the women's center who will be in contact with the public, either face to face or by telephone, must be selected carefully and be fully oriented to the philosophy and purpose of the center. Because so many women will have their first contact with the center by calling for information or an appointment, telephone receptionists need to be especially well trained and able to relate positively and quickly to women.

Being first with any new program or service is always an asset. But being perceived as special and unique, even though the hospital enters the market late, can be equally beneficial. Carefully assess the competition to determine the options available when creating an image. At times, this may be difficult for hospital employees, as there is a tendency to discount anything and everything the competition does. There is also the tendency mentioned earlier to simply copy what the competition has done. This will reinforce the image of the hospital as a follower, not a leader. Outside consulting assistance may be helpful to objectively evaluate competitive programs and assess the hospital's strengths and special opportunities in order to develop an image that will appeal to and attract women.

Innovative Services

Following is a list of programs frequently offered in an outpatient women's health care center. Each type of program lists several options for providing service. It is not necessary to provide all of the options listed in order to have an effective program.

1. *breast exam and disease detection*

   - education
   - self-examination instruction

- mammography and other diagnostic procedures
- information on surgical options

2. *osteoporosis testing*

   - education
   - bone densometer testing/screening
   - exercise programs
   - research

3. *premenstrual syndrome*

   - diagnosis and screening (both physical and psychological)
   - education on diet/lifestyle changes
   - support therapy groups
   - individual and family counseling
   - intervention

4. *alcohol and substance abuse (including smoking)*

   - diagnosis
   - education
   - support therapy groups
   - individual and family counseling
   - intervention
   - outpatient treatment or cosponsorship with other established community groups

5. *eating disorders*

   - diagnosis and testing
   - education
   - support therapy groups
   - individual and family counseling
   - inpatient treatment

6. *special diet and exercise*

- education and classes
- weight control programs
- cooking classes and nutritional guidance
- exercise programs for various age groups and physical conditions

7. *self-improvement and lifestyle changes*

- classes and educational programs for personal and professional growth and development:

  —stress management
  —career planning
  —assertiveness training
  —image development and enhancement
  —menopause and aging

8. *resource center and library*

- a room featuring publications and information of special interest to women, including:

  —tapes
  —journals
  —magazines
  —books
  —clipping service

9. *support therapy groups*

- interaction and support groups for women experiencing psychosocial problems, including:

  —death of a spouse or child
  —terminal disease

—divorce
—caregiver to a spouse or other relative
—aging

10. *referral services*

  • providing assistance in locating physicians or other health
    care resources

11. *programs involving treatment**

  • cosmetic surgery
  • laser GYN surgery
  • adolescent gynecology
  • infertility and genetics counseling

*These programs can be offered at the outpatient women's center
(with special equipment available to all attending medical staff) or
patients can be referred to physicians participating in the referral
system.

Chapter 12

Inpatient Services

12

Inpatient care for women is an area of opportunity that almost all acute care hospitals have, and one that almost none are utilizing. Inpatient women's care involves providing care to a particular group of women patients on one specially designed and decorated unit or wing in the hospital. Providing special inpatient services for women is relatively simple and inexpensive to implement.

The physical plant needs to be designed with all private rooms (or only one to two semiprivate rooms) decorated in contemporary colors to create a sophisticated, feminine environment. The style of decor is carried out in the carpeting, draperies, bed linens, napkins, towels, and special amenities throughout the unit and in each room. Space in the unit can be made available for the following support functions:

- patient dining room
- education and conference room
- gift shop
- hair and nail salon
- treatment room

Other special features on this unit include:

- daily newspaper
- a la carte menu with lighter fare

- fresh flower on breakfast or dinner tray
- guest trays for the family members
- color coordinated terry cloth robes and slippers
- buffet dining services in the patient dining room
- massage services
- business services:
    —typewriter
    —computer hook-up
    —dictaphone
    —photocopy services
    —special telephone line
    —secretarial assistance
- patient assistant/support person
- rapid admission service
- same day admissions
- postdischarge follow-up telephone call or home visit

Individual patient rooms are decorated in complementary colors and style, coordinated with the overall decor of the unit. The use of soft pastel colors with patterned wallpaper, elegant prints, and personal toiletry items combines to create a comfortable hotel-like space. Furniture should be compatible with the decorating scheme and include a comfortable lounge chair and reading lamp in each room. Space and furniture for family members, as well as eating and sleeping accommodations for a husband or support person, should be included in patient rooms.

A women's inpatient unit can house the following types of patients:

- gynecological surgery patients
- breast surgery patients
- other general surgery patients
- cosmetic surgery patients
- clean medical (female) patients

Without wishing to appear discriminatory, this unit will be more successful if certain types of patients are not admitted. It is recommended that the following types of patients be admitted to other medical-surgical floors:

- chronic or terminally ill patients
- disoriented patients
- male patients
- very elderly patients

STAFF REQUIREMENTS

The nursing staff needs to be responsive to women and to be service oriented. Professional staff must be carefully chosen and trained. The care and service offered needs to be provided with the same philosophy that underlies family-centered maternity care. This approach focuses on attending to the needs of the patient as an individual, and is responsive to psychosocial, as well as physical, needs. All of the staff needs to be knowledgeable and well informed about women's health care. The staff will also need additional training and ongoing education to be skilled in both medical and surgical nursing.

As noted in Chapter 10, women are more interested in information about health care and disease than are men. In response to this, additional education programs will be an asset to this service. It is helpful to hire or assign a patient educator the responsibility for developing and coordinating all patient education classes and outreach activities associated with this unit. Many of the programs can be provided in conjunction with an outpatient women's center. Lectures, written materials, and videotapes should address specific concerns of women, including:

- coping with menopause
- coping with breast surgery
- techniques for breast self-examination
- smoking cessation

- biofeedback and headaches
- nutritional education and diet
- safe exercise after surgery

One way to ensure proper integration and coordination among all the women's health care programs and services is to have one product line manager for both inpatient and outpatient women's health care. As noted in Chapter 11, this person needs to have significant latitude over decision making in regard to these programs and should report to a member of the top administrative staff. This position is not a nursing position, but rather a midlevel management position. Therefore, the product line coordinator should report to a senior operations executive in the hospital.

MARKETING AND PROMOTION

If the hospital decides to develop both an inpatient and outpatient service, marketing and promotional materials need to reflect the same image. Consistency in design and colors will be important to create identity between the two services. If the hospital decides to develop only a women's inpatient unit, all of the issues discussed in Chapter 11 still require consideration.

Patient educators for both inpatient and outpatient programs can assist in promotion by offering presentations to local women's organizations and civic groups. A slide presentation with a well-planned narrative focusing on the special philosophy and unique services of these programs will be useful in creating community awareness and interest.

Following are three case studies that illustrate some of the principles described above. The first case study focuses on an inpatient unit for women at Fort Myers Community Hospital, Fort Myers, Florida. To the authors' knowledge, it is one of few facilities that has developed this type of unit so completely.

The second case study describes the program at Woman's Hospital of Texas in Houston, Texas. This is a variation in the approach to provide a special service orientation to women.

Finally, the third case study focuses on St. Joseph's Hospital in Lowell, Massachusetts. This hospital is developing a comprehensive inpatient and outpatient women's center within the acute care facility. The unit is now under construction and will be completed in December 1987.

Case Study 1

Fort Myers Community Hospital, Fort Myers, Florida

Fort Myers Community Hospital is a 400-bed, acute care hospital which has provided health care to the Fort Myers community for twelve years. The hospital is a full service facility, with special services available in cardiac care, ophthalmology, and oncology. No obstetrical services are available.

This case study focuses on the Women's Pavilion, a 62-bed unit that offers care for practically any illness or surgical need a woman may encounter. The Women's Pavilion is located in one wing on the second floor of the hospital and has twenty-four semiprivate rooms, thirteen private rooms, and one VIP suite. It was the hospital's wish to create only private rooms, but because of a high demand for admission to this unit during the winter season, semiprivate rooms are a necessity. The entire unit is decorated in contemporary colors and furnishings, with coordinated curtains, wallpaper, and bed linens.

The Women's Pavilion program embraces a new philosophy in patient care—one that meets each woman's needs on an individual basis—whether physical, emotional, or psychosocial. Much emphasis is placed on education, both preventive and relevant to each individual patient's condition. The additional cost for care on this unit is ten dollars per day above the standard hospital charges. The one VIP suite available costs one hundred dollars per day above the charge for a private room on the Women's Pavilion.

Special services and amenities include the following:

- A writing tablet and pen are given to each patient in an embossed folder.
- An amenity kit (shampoo, lotion, hairspray, deodorant, and shower cap) is provided in a zippered bag.
- A special gown (with an elasticized neckline) and matching bed jacket are provided.
- A masseuse is available ten hours per day.
- A special gourmet menu is available, with the option of ordering at other than mealtimes.
- Guest trays can be ordered from the gourmet menu.
- A full-time diet clerk oversees quality and resolves menu problems, including special requests.
- There is a pantry available to all patients, with yogurt, ice cream, snack foods, and a wide selection of juices and beverages.
- Continental breakfasts (danish, coffee, and newspaper) are available as early as 6:00 A.M.
- There is no charge for television or telephones.
- Secretarial services are available and include any of the following:
  —typewriter
  —dictaphone
  —copy machine
  —personal computer
- An educational resource room is available for patient use, with books, magazines, cassettes, and a national clipping service that provides current articles.

- STAR (straight to a room) admission is used for all patients. They are taken immediately to their room and admission papers and procedures are completed there.
- A short-stay (less than twenty-four hours) program is available for cosmetic surgery patients. Surgery is performed in the physician's office; the patient then comes to the unit to spend from several hours to an entire night recovering.

The hospital offers these amenities for a reason beyond marketing. The staff firmly believe that a woman's response to treatment is "infinitely faster in such surroundings."

The concept was developed as part of the hospital's overall strategy for creating new product lines. The choice of women's health care was based upon an awareness of national trends in women's health care and a market assessment that included analysis of demographic data and a consumer opinion survey. The market analysis showed that fifty-four percent of the population was female, with twenty-two percent being sixty-five years or older and another twenty-two percent aged seventeen years or younger.

Hospital administration believed an opportunity existed with either age group. But they decided the greatest opportunity would come by targeting specific consumers: women thirty-five years of age or older who had not previously been a patient. The hospital did not want to displace its current patients, but it did want to increase its market share by attracting specific consumers who had never been admitted there before.

Once the decision was made to make women's health care a product line, a women's health care task force was formed. It was chaired by the vice president of nursing and included vice presidents and directors from the following departments:

- medical/surgical nursing
- materials management
- food service
- support services
- marketing
- environmental services
- plant operations
- admitting/patient accounts

In addition, the hospital formed two community advisory committees. One committee was composed entirely of business women considered to be opinion leaders in Fort Myers. The second committee was composed of physician's wives married to key admitters or politically influential attending medical staff members. Hospital administration believed that the women in these two groups represented the type of patient they wished to attract.

The women's health care task force met with the two committees in informal focus group discussions to gather input on the services and amenities that would make the Women's Pavilion special. The program was built on their suggestions, even to the colors chosen for the unit. The committees also met with task force members to review plans as the project progressed.

Following the initial meetings with the two committees, task force members met and discussed all of the suggestions provided. Each member was then assigned responsibility for two or three of the suggestions. Members were to work out a plan for implementation and then report solutions back to the group.

Because the hospital is part of a larger corporation, the project needed a strong commitment from management at both the hospital and corporate level. Having received corporate support, the hospital's president made this project a top priority.

The Women's Pavilion was promoted through the use of an attractive brochure describing the unit and its special services. Considerable media attention was received because of the uniqueness of the program.

The outcomes of the program indicate that the hospital's goals have been achieved. One year after opening, an informal audit showed that forty-nine percent of the patients on the unit had not previously been admitted to the hospital. Volume has increased by ten to twenty percent in the summer months, traditionally the hospital's period of lowest census.

Another benefit of the program is the pride all employees feel about having such a unique service. There is a belief that development of the Women's Pavilion has enhanced standards throughout the hospital. Other floors are now going through a renovation process and the special staff selection and orientation process is being utilized as services are upgraded and additional new product lines developed.

Future plans call for implementation of an osteoporosis program and the possible development of a comprehensive outpatient women's health care program.

Case Study 2

Woman's Hospital of Texas, Houston, Texas

Woman's Hospital of Texas opened in 1976. The hospital was developed by a group of physicians who wished to provide services in a facility dedicated to women. The hospital is currently owned by Hospital Corporation of America (HCA) and offers a full complement of inpatient services for women. Outpatient care, including a fitness center, menopausal center, and educational programs, is also provided.

This case study focuses on the special amenities available to patients who are willing to pay an additional fee. Six private luxury suites are available in the hospital: three on the maternity care floor and three on a gynecology floor. The decor of the rooms is done in contemporary pastel colors with coordinated wallpaper and bed linens.

The program, called the Cameo Experience, is designed to provide special services and amenities to any patient who chooses to be hospitalized in one of these rooms. The additional cost for care in a cameo room is one hundred dollars per day.

Some of the special services and amenities included are the following:

- Special menu for meals (patients can also order hors d'oeuvres if desired).
- Silk flowers are provided on meal trays.
- A newspaper is delivered each morning.
- A robe with the hospital's logo is provided during the hospital stay.
- Stationery and stamped envelopes are provided.
- A masseuse is available in-house twenty-four hours per day.
- Beautician services are available if desired.
- Limousine services for the drive home are available.
- A resource library is available in the hospital.

On the maternity care unit, patients are provided these additional amenities:

- a cameo ring for the baby
- a framed photograph of the baby
- a car seat

The concept was developed from an idea submitted by an employee (a male business manager). It was motivated by high demand for the VIP rooms in the hospital. Initially, only one room was planned on the maternity care unit. However, physicians and patient demand supported the development of additional rooms. When the hospital developed the service, it was assumed that the major users of these rooms would be high-income, private patients. However, they have found that the biggest users, especially on the maternity care unit, are blue collar families who want "the best" for their childbirth experience.

The idea was given to the marketing committee of the hospital. This committee established a subcommittee chaired by the employee who originated the idea. The other members of the subcommittee were representatives of each department that would be affected by implementation of the concept. The subcommittee began by listing all the possible amenities they thought they would like if hospitalized. Then the chairman of the subcommittee worked with each departmental representative to determine how each special feature could be delivered. A primary goal of the subcommittee was to increase service without increasing cost over what could reasonably be recovered from the patient. The cost for all of the amenities offered is covered in the additional charge per day.

The cameo rooms were promoted through the use of a special brochure describing the rooms and the special services. In addition, the hospital received media coverage because of the uniqueness of the program in the Houston area.

Since initiating the program, occupancy in the rooms has been at seventy percent. The hospital will increase the number of rooms as demand dictates. Administration does not believe the rooms have attracted any new patients. They do believe, however, that the program increases options and better satisfies existing patients. Questionnaires from patients support the fact that the program enhances the hospital experience and has been enthusiastically received.

Case Study 3

St. Joseph's Hospital, Lowell, Massachusetts

St. Joseph's Hospital is a 232-bed, acute care facility that has provided care to Lowell and the surrounding communities for more than a century. The hospital is a full service facility located in the inner city.

This case study focuses on the Women's Pavilion, which will occupy the entire fifth floor of the hospital. The floor is currently under construction. When completed, the Pavilion will include a ten-bed single-room maternity care unit, a seventeen-bed inpatient women's unit, and an outpatient women's center located between the two inpatient units. A brief description of each area follows.

The single-room maternity care unit is designed to provide care for one thousand patients per year. The unit has eight private childbearing rooms, two private ante-partum/postpartum rooms, and two traditional delivery rooms for complicated or cesarean deliveries. Each patient room is designed with a private bathroom and shower. In addition, space is provided for the following support functions:

- well-baby nursery with infant stabilization, isolation, and procedure rooms

- admitting office
- equipment and clean utility room
- soiled utility room
- patient education/dining room
- family waiting room
- anesthesia workroom
- staff conference room
- nurses' station
- nurses' lounge and locker/change room
- physicians' lounge and locker/change room
- physicians' on-call rooms
- staff offices

As indicated in Chapter 5, this single-room maternity care unit will provide innovative maternity care options as well as traditional maternity care. Each patient will be admitted directly to a private childbearing room and, barring complications or a desire for traditional care, will remain in one room for labor, delivery, recovery, and postpartum care.

The women's inpatient unit is composed of seventeen private rooms and will provide care to the following types of patients:

- GYN surgery patients
- breast surgery patients
- general surgery patients
- clean medical patients

All of the patient rooms are private, with space available in each for husband or support person to eat and sleep. All of the rooms have a private bath; however, eleven rooms are designed with a shower shared between two patient rooms. In addition, the following support functions are included:

- patient/family kitchen
- patient education/dining room
- gift shop
- nurses' station
- beauty salon
- utility room

Some of the special amenities planned for patients include:

- daily newspapers
- writing paper and stamped envelopes
- color coordinated robes
- a fresh flower on the breakfast tray
- gourmet menu
- guest trays for family
- hair and nail care
- direct admission to patient's room

The outpatient women's center is designed to provide services primarily to women who are not hospitalized. However, patients from both the maternity care unit and inpatient women's unit will have access to the center. The purpose of the center will be to provide services that respond to the total needs (physical, psychosocial, and emotional) of women. The center will engage in the following functions:

1. diagnosis, testing, and screening procedures
2. education and support therapy
3. health promotion

Services planned for development, based on market research of women living in the community, include:

- special exercise programs
- special diet programs
- osteoporosis screening
- mammography
- laser GYN surgery
- self-improvement classes

In addition, a resource library with books, magazines, cassettes, and other educational materials will be provided.

The plan for a Women's Pavilion was developed and initiated following a market area analysis providing research on maternity care and other women's health care. The research was motivated by a steadily declining obstetric volume and the need to recruit new physicians. The entire floor had at one time housed the obstetrical department. Initially the hospital had planned only to renovate one wing for the new maternity care unit. The remaining space was to be utilized as a traditional medical/surgical floor.

Following consultation with a women's health care consulting firm, the decision was made to utilize the entire floor to develop the Women's Pavilion. A nurse from within the hospital was selected as director and assigned responsibility for managing the project.

In addition, an advisory committee of women from Lowell and the surrounding communities was created to provide input and information to the director.

At this time, renovation is in progress with a completion date in late 1987. Marketing materials, staff selection and training, and promotional plans are all in progress. Enthusiasm among hospital employees is high and community interest strong. However, until the Pavilion is open, goals and objectives cannot be measured.

A physical plant design that accommodates this type of program consolidation provides a number of significant benefits. Some of the benefits are:

- increased operational efficiencies such as staffing, information center, and resource library
- visual reinforcement of the hospital's commitment to women
- all three services can be marketed in one promotional package; in fact, the geographical proximity of each of the programs serves to increase patient/visitor awareness of the others
- a common location for all three programs enhances convenience for physicians and visitors

Obviously, not all facilities will have adequate space to develop a unit with all services combined in one location. However, when this can be accomplished, an ideal situation is created. Benefits will accrue from some combination of services, even if full integration cannot be achieved.

Part IV

Internal Marketing

Chapter 13

Guest Relations: Expanding Roles, Increasing Service

13

Until very recently, hospital administrators gave little consideration to the environment outside their institution. Consideration of
external environments was not necessary to managing a successful
hospital. Being competitive meant having equipment and services
comparable to the hospital across town or down the street. The
customer was the physician, and as long as he or she was happy, the
beds were full. Most third party payors paid rates that at least
covered costs. The press was the administrator's friend and the
business community his supporter. Neither interfered with how the
institution was operated.

Today, health care is delivered in a dynamic and highly competitive business climate. Significant change in reimbursement
mechanisms, the development of determinative delivery systems
(payors and providers), escalating malpractice litigation, and an
increasingly more vigilant press and business community create
pressures the hospital administrator must manage successfully if
the institution is to survive.

One of the most significant changes confronting the health care
industry is the prominent and growing role of the patient in the
selection of a hospital for care. Recent consumer surveys indicate
that the majority of decisions about choice of hospital are made by
the patient or by the patient in collaboration with his or her physician. Studies also show that women play a very prominent role in all
health care decisions. Women either make or influence sixty-seven
percent of all health care decisions.[1]

In today's competitive environment, the hospital's image and reputation weigh significantly in consumer choice. Patient satisfaction with the hospital contributes strongly to the establishment of image and reputation in the minds of the public. Because women use health care services in greater numbers than do men, their opinions and feelings about hospital experiences will color community perception about a particular hospital's image and reputation.

The public forms its perception of a hospital's image and reputation very differently than does the medical community. Because of a lack of the necessary knowledge or experience to objectively evaluate the differences in clinical care, the average consumer assumes that most hospitals provide good, quality clinical services. This is a given. Patient satisfaction, then, is built on other criteria:

- cleanliness
- contemporary, pleasant surroundings
- privacy
- safe, convenient parking
- special services and programs

However, by far the most important of these criteria is the manner in which the patient is treated by hospital staff. This is a particularly important factor for women. Repeatedly, women rank "professional, caring nurses" as number one when asked to list their reasons for choosing a hospital.

The attitudes and behaviors of hospital staff make a profound impression on women when they or family members are hospitalized. This is what they speak about when they discuss their experience with friends and acquaintances. And this is what most prominently comes to mind when women form their perceptions of a hospital's image and reputation.

Unfortunately, many hospital employees and even some hospital administrators do not understand that the definition of *quality patient care* has expanded to include this caring, concerned, personalized attention valued by all patients and their families. Many caregivers still consider their job to be only the delivery of excellent clinical care. No longer is this enough. The role of the modern health care worker (both clinical and support staff) is to respond fully to the needs of the individual patient. Hospital employees must perform clinical and technical tasks well, and they must also address the patients' psychosocial, emotional and spiritual needs.

In light of the recent staffing reductions and salary freezes, this often presents an almost overwhelming challenge. However, implementation of this new, expanded definition of quality must be an essential part of the hospital's marketing program. To the patient, the hospital employee *is* the hospital. Therefore, the manner in which the patient and his or her family and friends are treated by all employees is the single most powerful factor influencing the consumer's perception of the hospital.

The positive influence of a successful promotional campaign and even the impact of a respected physician's recommendation can be negated by the insensitive actions of hospital staff. All too often, women tell hospitals on consumer surveys and evaluation forms that they were satisfied with their clinical care, but not with the service they received. Their most common complaints involve:

- rude employees
- poor telephone manners
- sloppy appearance of employees
- lack of promptness in attending to the patients' needs
- disinterest in patients' fears, concerns, and wishes
- failure to provide adequate information in response to the patients' questions

Complaints such as these must be resolved for the hospital to establish and/or preserve the image and reputation necessary to increase market share. Therefore, internal marketing (i.e., the process of creating a caring, concerned attitude in all hospital staff) must be an integral part of the hospital's overall marketing program. If this component is not in place and functioning well, advertising and marketing dollars will net little long-term return.

Internal marketing or guest relations (as it is frequently called) has two purposes:

1. To make the hospital employee aware of the need for responsive, empathetic service as well as technically skillful care.
2. To provide the motivation, training, and support for attitude
   and behavior change that must occur to ensure delivery of this
   expanded quality of care.

The first purpose for internal marketing is very important and
often overlooked in many guest relations programs. Because the
pressures of a changing environment are part of the daily affairs of
hospital executives, they often assume that employees at all levels of
the organization are aware of how the health care industry has
changed. Frequently, this is not so. Before employees can commit
themselves to attitude and behavior changes, they must understand
the need to do so, and believe the changes are necessary.

Thus, the first step in any internal marketing program is education. Describing the changes in the industry, explaining how health
care purchasing decisions are made, and providing feedback from
patients about the care they value will help employees recognize that
their roles must expand.

Internal marketing has a number of components. First and fore-
most, top management and the board must believe in the value of
the individual employee, and accept and support the expanded
definition of quality. This commitment must be demonstrated
through allocation of resources (time and dollars) to internal marketing efforts. Through their words *and* actions, management must
communicate this support to employees. Simply talking about the
importance of a guest relations program or merely giving lip service
to this philosophy of care will ultimately result in failure. Without a
significant display of support from administration and the board,
even the best designed guest relations program will produce only
limited results.

Each internal marketing effort must be designed to reflect the
character of the institution and address the specific problems and
issues facing the hospital. Although many packaged programs offer
a good base from which to begin, they often are not tailored to reflect
the hospital's internal and external environment. To determine
specific issues to be addressed, an assessment of the contact mecha-

nisms contributing to the hospital's image should be examined. Some contacts to be examined are:

- telephone contacts
- evaluation forms and surveys
- written communication with the public

Information discovered through this audit can be used to orient staff to the need for change. This information will also identify the skills and training needed to achieve the required changes.

Providing staff with the training for strong interpersonal communication skills is the foundation of any internal marketing effort. To bring about the desired behavior change, all staff, regardless of the amount of contact they have with patients, must receive this basic training. Employees with significant patient contact require even more intensive training. The latter group should not be limited to physicians and nurses but also support staff, such as business office personnel, admitting staff, housekeepers, food service workers, telephone operators, gift shop workers, and volunteers.

For many hospitals, the formal internal marketing program ends when a training program has been completed. If real attitude and behavior changes are to occur, skill training is just the beginning. It must be followed by the development of goals and plans for applying new skills on a day-to-day basis. These are best developed in collaboration between each employee and his or her supervisor, reinforced by goals and objectives established to measure progress hospitalwide.

Ongoing evaluation is the important next step, for it measures performance against targets and creates motivation for behavior change. Hospitals with successful guest relations programs often incorporate internal marketing objectives into performance expectations for their employees. In this way, progress is reviewed regularly at the time of the employee's performance evaluation, and compensation can be made at least partially dependent upon the employee's proven ability to relate successfully to patients and other guests.

Although all change is difficult, change in behavior is easier to effect than change in attitude. If the hospital is serious about its commitment to internal marketing and ties compensation to performance, employees will make behavior changes to protect their jobs and/or increase their earnings. However, behavior changes without the commitment to develop a nurturing, supportive relationship with those served ultimately do not promote the image the hospital is striving to achieve with the guest relations program. Patients sense the lack of commitment and often interpret staff behavior as patronizing or manipulative.

Educating staff to the need for and importance of a new attitude can begin the process of attitudinal change. However, education alone will not be enough to sustain the process. Employees must also see and hear management at all levels support the change. Even with this hospitalwide show of support, more effort is necessary to cause attitudinal change.

To make lasting changes, staff must be rewarded and recognized continually and frequently for their good work and accomplishments. Recognition can come through articles in hospital publications or community newspapers that highlight the achievements of individuals, regular recognition awards for good performance, and special rewards (e.g., theater tickets, parties, complimentary dinners) for overall hospital success.

However, the most lasting recognition comes from daily acknowledgment by administration of the value and importance of each employee to the hospital. This acknowledgment is expressed through reasonable staffing levels and work schedules; pleasant, comfortable spaces for staff to relax and eat; service benefits like discounts on food or special programs offered by the hospital; and fair compensation for work performed. Today, hospitals are asking employees to give more and do it with a smile. Almost all employees have difficulty giving back what they perceive is not received. If they feel valued and supported, they are willing to give concern and recognition to their patients. This basic exchange is the heart of all truly successful internal marketing efforts.

NOTE

1. Joe Inquanzo and Mark Harju, "Creating a Market Niche," *Hospitals,* January 1, 1985.

The Hospital/Physician Connection

14

Another important variable in the hospital's overall marketing strategy is the physician. Although patients are taking a much more active role in selecting a hospital, the physician's opinion still has significant influence in a patient's choice of hospital. Many programs, especially those for women, link the hospital and the physician together in the patient's mind. Thus, what one does reflects upon the other.

Making program changes and promoting an attitude of sensitive, personalized care must come out of the partnership between the hospital and the medical staff. Often this partnership does not exist. The hospital is struggling to satisfy patients and increase volumes. The physician also wants to satisfy patients, but may do so in a way that does not support the hospital. If both hospital and physician are not working for the same end in the same way, the positive changes implemented in hospital programs and staff attitudes will be negated. For example, in an innovative single-room maternity care system, pediatricians examine babies in the mother's room. This component of single-room maternity care is highly valued by maternity care patients. The hospital can create an environment supportive of this service by renovating the mother's room to make this procedure possible and effective. But if the physicians refuse to examine the baby in the room, this desired service cannot be provided.

THE NECESSITY FOR COMPARABLE STANDARDS

Office staff employed by physicians must also enter into the partnership. If staff manifest behavior that is uncaring and insensitive, patients will seek treatment elsewhere, resulting in the loss of the patient not just to the physician, but possibly to the hospital as well. For example, if the hospital develops a new program for women, such as cosmetic surgery, and markets it heavily in the community, patients responding to this program will call the hospital for information or treatment. The hospital will refer the patient to one of the attending physicians involved with the program. If this physician or his or her staff do not treat the patient in a positive manner, all of the money and time the hospital spent in developing and marketing the program will be lost.

Physicians are just beginning to acknowledge the power of interpersonal relationships, especially in regard to patients. Many physicians still believe they can compensate with knowledge and position. However, women in large numbers indicate they will switch physicians if they do not like the manner in which they are treated by a doctor, a partner in the practice, or the office staff.

To create an effective partnership, physicians and their staff must be educated in much the same way, and on similar topics, as hospital staff. This task often becomes the responsibility of the hospital because physicians are having difficulty accepting the changes occurring in the health care environment. These changes are threatening their previous pre-eminence, increasing legal exposure, and compromising their past position of control.

EDUCATING PHYSICIANS

As with hospital staff, education for physicians and office staff must focus on attitude and behavior change. To make the required changes, knowledge is essential, especially in two broad areas:

1. *Hospital Goals.* Physicians must understand:

   • what the hospital is doing and why

- what the hospital expects to accomplish and when it will be done
- what the physician's role will be in carrying out these objectives

2. *Private Practice Goals.* Physicians must understand:

- what can be done to build and strengthen their individual practices
- how to go about accomplishing this goal

In order to bring about any change, it is important that the players clearly recognize the benefits that will occur once the changes are implemented. Physicians are no different in this respect. To encourage physicians to modify and change individual behaviors and practice methods, the hospital can provide assistance by offering a program on medical practice marketing to its attending staff. This type of program will provide physicians with the tools needed to identify strengths and weaknesses as well as methods to enhance patient satisfaction.

Attitude change is necessary for true behavior change. But changing attitudes is far more difficult than changing behaviors. Physicians will have some built-in prejudices that will make it difficult for them to commit to change. Some ways to help physicians recognize the need for change are:

- Provide statistics that verify declining physician activity as well as hospital admissions.
- Provide objectively gathered and analyzed public opinions of consumer preferences and feelings about the attending medical staff.
- Provide case histories of successful changes implemented by other hospitals and their medical staff.
- Give physicians the opportunity to make site visits to successful programs and speak with their peer group.

Pressures in the hospital environment have had a tendency to further polarize physicians and management, thus increasing adversarial situations. As a result, many hospital administrators feel resentful about the need to provide the recognition and rewards necessary to effect behavior and attitudinal changes in physicians. Yet, any realistic attempt to create change must involve recognition and reward. Physicians are still one of the hospital's most important consumer groups. Hospital administrators must strike the balance between courting and cursing the physician in such a way as to create a viable partnership where neither dominates and both win. Leadership in creating this partnership usually falls to hospital administration. Some of the most frequently heard needs physicians indicate would be appreciated and demonstrate recognition are

- participation in program planning and program evaluation
- amenities that make their lives easier and more pleasant:
  —adequate locker space
  —attractive, comfortable lounge space
  —private bathrooms and showers for men and women
  —private on-call rooms
  —convenient eating facilities with good, quality food available 24 hours per day
  —convenient parking
- having an equitable referral system
- having reasonable surgery schedules
- timely information available on hospital activities, especially new programs or staff
- assistance in enhancing their practices:
  —practice assessment
  —practice management
  —practice marketing
  —recruiting new partners
- inclusion in hospital promotions when appropriate

EDUCATING ADMINISTRATORS

As stated previously, in order for both internal and external marketing programs to be effective, a commitment must be clearly and openly made by the top management team. Simply talking about support, without visible commitment to such programs, will not provide sufficient evidence of management's support and may work to undermine the projects.

In order for top management to offer meaningful support, they too must be educated. In the past, hospital administrators operated in a sheltered environment and from a perspective limited to the health care industry. Now administrators are forced to operate in a competitive business climate and perform like corporate executives. Because this change has been so rapid, many administrators have not developed the required broader perspective. Much of this perspective involves not only a business approach to health care, but also recognition and adaptation to the changes occurring in society.

As noted previously, one of the most important changes that has occurred in the past ten years involves the expanding role of women in our society. Effects of this change have had significant impact on the health care industry. It is now known that women play a far greater role in health care decisions than do men. It is also known that the behavior of health care providers greatly affects the choices women make. For health care administrators to better understand and adjust to this change, increased information in the following areas is often helpful:

- To become familiar with and understand how women make choices and evaluate health care providers.
- To understand *and* acknowledge the ways women perceive themselves in view of the changes that have occurred in society (both female patients and female staff).
- To fully understand and appreciate how a service orientation is defined by women (e.g., addressing the patient by the name she prefers or knocking on the door before entering a patient room).

Opportunities for education used to occur informally as hospital administrators exchanged information with their peers. Today, because of the increased competition, this informal exchange of information takes place much less frequently. Therefore, each administrator must seek information through more structured channels or through unconventional means. The methods are similar to those described earlier for physicians. They include:

- conducting public opinion surveys and focus group activities with previous patients and potential patients
- making site visits and having meetings with administrators at hospitals in a distant community (if the administrator is not in the service area, he or she will welcome the opportunity to brag and share marketing strategies and operational details)
- attending special education programs that focus on national trends and current issues in the women's health care industry
- reading current health care and other business literature to stay abreast of social and business changes (rather than relying solely on staff to supply ideas and information)
- talking with staff regularly to:
  —exchange ideas
  —brainstorm about changes that are occurring in the marketplace
  —strategize about ways the hospital can maximize on these changes

These suggestions may seem very elementary. However, there are few administrators or senior managers who actively do these things or even think about doing them.

Managers in successful programs have indicated that without the active backing and support of the chief executive officer, program development would not have been accomplished as quickly or as well. The importance of the chief executive officer's role in facilitating change cannot be stressed enough. The role of this one individual is paramount to program success. From our perspective, this role includes:

- The ability to see and communicate the "big picture" as it relates to planned program change and product line development.

- The willingness to support and enforce change after commitment to do so has been made.
- The interest and time to show genuine concern for the adjustments that employees, physicians and patients must make when changes occur.
- The savvy to demonstrate leadership through behavior as well as words.

The physician/hospital connection requires support and recognition of motivational goals in order to be effective. Both physicians and hospitals desire success. Being successful in today's complex environment requires the ability to change and to support change within the organization. Developing comparable standards and practices while giving physicians, staff, and management the information needed to understand change will make the accomplishment of goals far less difficult and much more likely to occur.

Chapter 15
Conclusion

15

In the past, health care providers said quality performance could not be achieved because quality could not be defined. Thus the inability to define quality served as justification for failure to apply the discipline necessary to achieve quality performance. Quality is still thought to be too intangible to define, and every employee, physician and patient has a different definition for it. For example, today administrators and hospital staff define quality as more service and special amenities. Physicians and academicians define quality care in clinical terms relating to medical care. Because health care providers as a group are unable to agree on the definition of quality, they are reacting to the patients' definition: more service and special amenities. Service, as defined by patients, means friendly, responsive staff; personalized attention; and participation in decisions about their health care.

Much of this book has focused on the need for a service orientation that is reflected in the delivery and marketing of health care services to women. Without detracting from the importance of service, it should be noted that merely providing service or special amenities is not all that needs to be done. Service is only part of a much broader perspective about the changes that must occur in the provision of health care if hospitals are to survive.

In fact, service is part of an expanded definition of quality. Health care providers have always talked and worried about quality care. Today, it is necessary to talk and worry about quality performance.

Our definition of quality performance is performance without mistakes. The health care industry must develop and commit to an industry where mistakes are not accepted as part of the norm. Standards for performance that allow a 95 percent success rate establish the expectation for 95 percent, rather than 100 percent, performance. Mistakes do occur, but the difference in this concept is that slack (to accommodate error) is not automatically built into performance expectations. If health care providers say this cannot be done, they are giving license to mistakes being made.

Every hospital is looking for a way to distinguish itself in its community. Marketing plans and strategies are focused on creating and communicating distinction to the hospital's customers, both patients and physicians. Thus far, health care providers have attempted distinction in a fragmented and sporadic manner. In some programs (e.g., women's health care), hospitals are achieving distinction, while in others almost nothing is being done. The reason for this is that there has been no organizational standard for quality performance established by administration or the board. And yet quality performance is the one way to clearly distinguish one hospital from another.

To the authors' knowledge, only one hospital in the United States has implemented a quality performance program to achieve this end. NKC, Inc., in Louisville, Kentucky, began such a program in January 1986 by hiring four full-time staff members whose sole responsibility is quality improvement. Similar programs will undoubtedly be initiated as hospital administrators recognize the benefits and opportunities inherent in this approach to the provision of health care.

Hospitals can no longer dismiss this issue by saying a standard for quality cannot be developed because quality cannot be defined. This argument will no longer hold. Service industries in this country and other countries have managed to achieve quality performance. Hospital administrators must now do the following:

1. Apply the discipline necessary to define quality in operational terms.
2. Commit to the standards of quality as defined.
3. Enforce the standards to ensure quality performance.

In this way, quality becomes the product line that distinguishes the hospital in its marketplace. This is compatible with the hospital's goals to attract women and satisfy all patients. Quality thus becomes the foundation upon which all programs are built and marketed.

Index

About the Authors

Ruthie H. Dearing, MHSA, JD, is president of Dearing & Associates, Incorporated, a health care consulting firm, which provides specialized consulting services for the planning, design, and marketing of maternity and other women's health care programs. She received her JD from the Gonzaga University School of Law and her MHSA from Arizona State University. She has supervised program design and implementation for over 200 hospitals and free-standing health care institutions across the country. Ms. Dearing has been a frequent lecturer at medical conferences and has three other major publications on women's health care to her credit.

Helen A. Gordon, RN, CNM, is currently Director of Women-Infant Services at Wake Medical Center in Raleigh, North Carolina. She began her career as a clinical nurse midwife. She has also served as staff nurse, head nurse, and clinical nurse practitioner in various maternity programs and Director of Maternal Child Health Nursing at St. Mary's Hospital in Minneapolis. Ms. Gordon has been a contributor to the *Journal of Nurse Midwifery* and two textbooks on maternity care.

Dorolyn M. Sohner, RN, BSN, has been involved in women's health care since 1959. Following graduation with honors from the University of Minnesota, she began her career as a staff nurse at that institution's hospital affiliate and progressed to Clinical Director. She then served as Vice President of Patient Services at St. Francis

Regional Medical Center for seven years, prior to joining Dearing & Associates, where she is a Senior Consultant. She is an experienced presenter and co-author of the book *The Nursing Care of Children with Cancer.*

Lynne C. Weidel, MHA, currently serves as Senior Consultant for Dearing & Associates. Her varied experience includes positions as Vice President for Corporate Planning at Portland, Oregon's Metropolitan Hospitals, CEO of the Clackamas Health Care Consortium, and Director of Planning for A.E. Brim & Associates. She received her MHA from the University of Minnesota and her BA from the University of Delaware.